CHRISTIAN HEROES
of the
HOLOCAUST
THE RIGHTEOUS GENTILES

Also by Joseph J. Carr:
The Twisted Cross

Joseph J. Carr has also written many books
on electronics and computers

CHRISTIAN HEROES
of the
HOLOCAUST
THE RIGHTEOUS GENTILES

Joseph J. Carr

Bridge Publishing, Inc.
South Plainfield, NJ 07080

**Quotations from the following books
are used with permission:**

Kurt Gerstein: The Ambiguity of Good
   by Saul Friedlander, Alfred A. Knopf Publishers,
New York, 1969

Lest Innocent Blood Be Shed
   by Philip Hallie, Harper & Row, Colophon Books,
San Francisco

The Avenue of the Righteous
   by Peter Hellman, Atheneum Books, New York,
1980

**Christian Heroes of the Holocaust
The Righteous Gentiles**
© 1984 Joseph J. Carr
Printed in the United States of America
ISBN: 0-88270-582-2
Library of Congress Number: 85-070538
Bridge Publishing, Inc.
2500 Hamilton Blvd.
South Plainfield, NJ 07080

Dedication

It is all too easy for a gentile Christian youngster to grow up in America mildly anti-Semitic; hints from our culture, the words of adults, and even the teachings of some churches make it likely. I would like to dedicate this book to Frank and Dottie Wiesel, formerly of Norfolk, Virginia, who employed me while I attended Old Dominion University. They are a sensitive, loving and caring couple (even though Frank pretends to be gruff on occasion) who treated me like a member of the family—and were the first Jewish family I ever knew well. They taught me to reject cultural anti-Semitism and love a whole people.

—Joseph J. Carr
Arlington, Virginia

Table of Contents

Preface... ix

1 A Time of Jacob's Trouble 1

2 The Righteous Ones
  of the Nations of the World 9

3 Guns and Roses: Ona Simaite 17

4 City of Refuge . . .
  Where Goodness Happened 23

5 "That Wonderful Russian Nun" . . .
  Mother Maria of Paris............................... 39

6 Miracle in Denmark:
  The Night the Jews Disappeared.................... 63

7 Kurt Gerstein . . . God's Spy in the SS?.......... 77

8 Felix Kersten:
  The Man With the Miraculous Hands 105

9 The Henry Family 115
  and Mademoiselle Chaumat.

10 Sietske Postma................................... 129

11 The Unrighteous Gentiles 135

12 Epilogue.. 153

   Further Reading 181

   Appendix: Roll Call of the Righteous 185

Preface

Several years ago I began studying the Holocaust as a side interest in a study of Hitler's occultic religion. This effort showed me that only a few Christians extended a helping hand to refugee Jews during the seven terrible years of the Holocaust. The organized churches did very little to aid the Jews, and indeed, some actually abetted the Nazis. But a few individuals did reach out and help, and their stories are very beautiful. This book tells a few of those stories. It is a book about spiritual heroes and modern martyrs; it is a book on practical Christian ethics; and it is also a book of hope for the future of Jewish-Christian relations.

Several people helped me immensely in writing this book, and they are due special acknowledgment. I am grateful to Adina Drechsler, a young Israeli woman who provided material from Yad Vashem Library in Jerusalem. Also appreciated is Elizebeth Kiehl, a reference librarian in the Arlington County (Virginia) Library Central Branch, who helped me with Interlibrary Loan System problems; Miss Debbie

Johnson of Washington Bible College (Lanham, Maryland), who typed the first manuscript; Mrs. Heather Wells, a Messianic Jewish woman who read the manuscript and made comments; Bill and Willa Trifiatis, Bing Fuller, fellow writers Aggie Villaneuva, Debbie Lawrence, and Reverend David Shibley, and editor Drew Thomas, all of whom offered much encouragement. Last but most important, my wife Bonnie who provides the most encouragement of all and has the good grace to let me have the time to write.

Joseph J. Carr

Poem by Mother Maria to Protest the German "Yellow Star" Order

Two triangles, a star
The shield of King David, our forefather
This is election, not offence
The great path and not an evil

Once more is a term fulfilled
Once more roars the trumpet of the end
And the fate of a great people
Once more is by the prophet proclaimed

Thou art persecuted again, O Israel
But what can human ill will mean to thee,
Thee, who hast heard the thunder from Sinai?

1

A Time of Jacob's Trouble

Satan ran amuck in Europe during the Holocaust (1938-1945) and, in the process, murdered two thirds of European Jewry. Given the ruthless efficiency of the Nazi death engine, however, it is miraculous that *any* Jews at all survived! But more than 2.5 million Jews did survive. In the very furnace of the Nazi hell, one third of the intended victims escaped. According to Philip Friedman, author of *Their Brothers' Keepers,* survival was impossible without the active help of Christians. During those years, a few Christians—very few—walked right into the gates of Hell and snatched away Satan's victims.

The reaction of the gentile population in occupied nations to German demands for surrender of the Jews determined in some measure the success of the Nazi extermination program in that country. The force of public opinion was a power for the Germans to reckon with in most countries. In Denmark, for example, almost all of the people from King Christian X down to the common man on the street refused German demands. A story some historians consider apocryphal nevertheless illustrates Danish attitudes. When the Germans ordered Danish Jews to wear a yellow Star of David on their clothes so that they could be identified, King Christian responded by going out the next morning on a public horseback ride wearing the six-pointed star on his own clothes. In proud defiance of the Nazi order, his act proclaimed that any Dane was as good as any other. By that evening the streets of Copenhagen were full of gentile Danes wearing yellow Magen Davids. The Germans rescinded the yellow star order, and it never reappeared in Denmark.

The Germans scheduled the roundup of Denmark's Jews for deportation to the death camps on the evening of October 1, 1943 (Rosh Hashana that year). The Nazis knew that the Jews would be in their homes or synagogues celebrating the holiday—an easy catch. But a minor German diplomat who was dealing with the SS heard of the plans and tipped off the Danes. A Lutheran pastor and a Danish politician passed the word to as many others as they could locate, and they in turn passed the word to their Jewish friends. Throughout the day, gentile Danes hid almost all of the nation's Jewish population. Over the next few months, Christian Danes ferried the Jews out of the country in small boats to neutral Sweden where they passed the war in safety.

Poland and the Ukraine were different. In the Ukraine, the local populace often assisted the Germans in rounding up Jews, and on at least one occasion cheered SS (Schutzstaffel, literally "defense staff") firing squads as they executed Jews. Some Ukrainians later joined the SS and became concentration camp guards.

In Poland, the danger to a gentile hiding Jews was almost as great from other Poles as from the Germans. Anti-Semitism had a long and violent history in central Europe, so Polish anti-Semites didn't need the Germans to teach them how to kill Jews! Polish terrorists spread an anti-Semitic gospel of hatred even after the war was over. It was often the case that Polish saints who sheltered Jews were shot by local terrorist groups. After the war, a Polish peasant named Kicinski begged two Jews who had found refuge in his home during the occupation "please don't tell anyone, for I fear for my life if the story gets out."

But to keep events in proper perspective, we must understand the situation in Poland, and how it might have caused many frightened Christians to refuse when Jews asked for help. The situation in Poland and other "Occupied Eastern Territories" was very different from that in Denmark.

The Danes are racially related to the Germans. To Hitler, they personified the blond Nordic ideals of Nazi racial theory. The Germans tried to maintain the fiction that Denmark was not an "occupied nation" at all, but rather a "model protectorate." Until October 1943, when Danes finally rebelled over the German decision to deport Denmark's Jews to Auschwitz, the Nazis acted in Denmark a lot less brutally than they did in Poland. According to Nazi racial theory, the Slavic peoples of Poland were subhuman, only a step or two above the Jews, and thus fit only for slavery. From just hours after the invasion of Poland, the Germans behaved with unprecedented bestiality toward the Poles. When this horrible oppression was coupled in obscene unholy matrimony with native Polish anti-Semitism, the result was the Holocaust. Hitler found it easy to locate most of the death camps on Polish soil.

While the Polish reaction to the Holocaust was among the most despicable in Europe, there were also many saintly heroes and heroines among the Poles. Among the "Righteous Gentiles" recognized by the State of Israel for saving Jews during the Holocaust there are more Poles than any other nationality.

Hiding Jews was not the easy matter it may seem from the safe perspective of decades later. The Germans had a policy of summary execution of gentiles who aided the Jews in even the simplest ways. In most cases, the Christian who helped a Jew was either shot on the spot or hauled to the nearest street corner or public square and hanged. Often as not, the body of the executed victim was left hanging as a lesson to other gentiles who might be tempted to aid a Jew. A "lucky" few were sent to the death camps where they had at least a slim chance of escape or survival.

Nor did the Nazis spare the families of the Christians who aided their Jewish brethren. The usual practice was to execute the wife, children and other members of the household along with the "guilty" person. When a Christian husband decided to take Jews into his home, or to aid them in any way whatsoever, he did so at the risk of the lives of those people he loved the most. The price for giving a Jew so much as a handful of bread crumbs was death in the most public manner possible.

It was not sufficient for a Christian to have courage (although that was an essential if undefinable characteristic) and the willingness to risk the lives of one's family; it was also necessary to have a properly camouflaged *mellina* (hiding place) where the Jews could live. Furthermore, it was necessary to have contacts with others who were also willing to share the risks and the work. These friends were necessary to increase the forewarning in the event of an impending raid, and to accept the Jewish refugees just before the raid actually took place.

The network of like-minded people was also needed because, as tragic experience throughout the war showed, survival required constant changes of hiding place; frequent moves between successive *mellinas* was essential. Most of the Jews who survived the war outside of the camps were in constant motion, never resting in any one place too long.

Many times Jews were discovered by sheer accident. But in too many cases, throughout Europe, they and their hosts were betrayed to the Nazis by informers. Whatever the motivation—money, food rations, anti-Semitism or just plain antagonism towards the host—informers accounted for a tragically large number of hiding Jews who were discovered by the Gestapo. At one time, the bounty for turning a Jew over to SS killers was four loaves of bread, or a little meat and a jar of marmalade!

The stories given in this book are some of the highlights of the much larger story of individual

Christians who risked their lives and the lives of their loved ones to be their brothers' keepers. While the institutional churches abetted Satan with their inappropriate silence, many individuals—Protestant, Roman Catholic and Eastern Orthodox—risked everything to save Jews from the Nazi death factories.

Many of the Righteous Gentiles were Roman Catholic priests, nuns and monks. The role of Pope Pius XII in the Holocaust has been criticized. But while "official" Vatican silence was lamentable, it was also understandable in view of the fact that Vatican City in Rome was totally surrounded by the German army. Individuals in the Roman Catholic religious community often defied the Nazis by aiding Jews, and evidence suggests that their activities had high-level—even Papal—approval. Some Roman Catholic convents were overrun with Jewish children camouflaged as gentiles—and some of those nuns attending the children had distinctly masculine features peeking out from behind their habits! By the end of the war, more than 5,000 priests, nuns and monks were killed for their part in countering the Holocaust. We Protestants have a habit of remembering our own heroes, while ignoring those of other Christian traditions. We remember Dietrich Bonhoeffer, but forget that there were also thousands of other saints in the concentration camps—people who didn't write essays for posterity, but whose heroism was every bit as great as those who are widely publicized.

The story of the Holocaust is a grim one, but the stories of the Righteous Gentiles are an uplifting moral change and are a profound study in Christian ethics. Some of those stories are told in the chapters to follow.

2

The Righteous Ones
of the Nations of the World

He who saves one life saves as it were the
whole world

—Babylonian Talmud

When the Nazi death engine rolled across Europe destroying dozens of thousand-year-old Jewish communities, it was aided both directly and indirectly by gentiles. The most contemptible, of course, were those who actively participated as informers, police and concentration camp guards. There were others, however, who did not directly participate in the slaughter but whose hands are nonetheless unclean because they remained silent when they could have spoken out, or they remained passive when they could have acted to take Jews out of harm's way.

Fortunately, there were a few gentiles—a precious few—who tore a hole in the Nazi night and helped save the remnant of Israel. Those few we call the "Righteous Gentiles."

The official title conferred upon those courageous people is "The Righteous Ones of the Nations of the World" (*Hasidei Ummot Ha-Olam* in Hebrew).

The title "Righteous Gentile" is granted by an agency of the State of Israel called "Yad Vashem"—The Heroes and Martyrs Remembrance Authority. This institution sits on a hillside in Jerusalem and serves as a monument to the murdered 6,000,000. The name "Yad Vashem" is taken from the Hebrew text of Isaiah 56:5 and eloquently sums up the charter of the institution: "a name and a place." Yad Vashem exists to give a name and a place to the nameless ones whose place in the world was torn from them by Nazi hatred.

At Yad Vashem there is a synagogue reminiscent of the humble *Shtetls* of Eastern Europe. A Hall of Records is there to record for history the names of the dead. Yad Vashem has a research center for scholars and a museum for visitors. There is a memorial—the Hall of Remembrance—on whose walls are inscribed the names of the twenty-two largest death camps (*Vernichtungslagers*) where two thirds of European Jewry vanished. An eternal flame in the Hall of Remembrance keeps alive their memory.

On a path that slopes gently away from Yad Vashem toward the parking lot there is a long row of small trees planted in honor of the Righteous Gentiles—"the Avenue of the Righteous." More than seven hundred trees have been planted, each one honoring a Righteous Gentile. Article 9 of the August 19, 1953, law that created Yad Vashem requires that the Righteous Ones of the Nations of the World also be given a name and a place; for them was created this avenue.

Who were these "Righteous Gentiles"? Although they seem to share certain characteristics, the Righteous Gentiles are a varied people. Very few were the sort of people one expects. They were not soldiers in the ordinary sense of the word, and they rarely had shown previous indications of great courage. Most were very ordinary people: a shopkeeper, a housewife, a nun who ran a soup kitchen for the poor of Paris, a pastor in a provincial backwater village, and a college librarian were typical of the lot. A common trait among these saints was that they were activists rather than theoreticians. Peter Hellman, writing in his book *The Avenue of the Righteous,* tells us about them:

> Action had to be the order of the day, however inconvenient or dangerous. Many of the Righteous, in fact, seem more adept at action than explanation. Asked why they did what they did, it is characteristic for them to shrug their shoulders and say, "I did nothing special. Anybody would have done it."

But not just "anybody" did it. Only a comparative handful responded in the selfless way required to earn the title "Righteous Gentile."

Candidates for the award are usually proposed by someone who knew of their deeds. Frequently it is one or more of the Jews who were saved by that person who proposes the candidacy; only rarely do candidates propose themselves. Modesty is among the most common traits of the candidates. A factor that sometimes hampers the official investigation is that most of the Righteous are not in the habit of promoting themselves.

Nominations come into Yad Vashem from all over the world. In many cases, the nominations come directly to Yad Vashem in Jerusalem, while in others they come from Israeli Embassies abroad. Each Embassy maintains a consular official whose duties include matters involving the Righteous Gentiles; some European embassies of Israel maintain several such officials.

A quasi-judicial committee chaired by a Justice of the Israeli Supreme Court reviews the nominations and conducts whatever investigation is needed to establish the facts. The process can take many years because it is difficult to ascertain the truth and certainty of events which passed unnoticed more than four decades previously. The committee requires strict adherence to judicial standards of evidence so as to ensure that the award is given only to those who merit it.

It was not sufficient for a candidate to have aided Jews; motive is a primary consideration. There are thousands of cases where Jews received help from gentiles at a cost. For example, there were along the borders between the occupied nations and their neutral neighbors many *passeurs* (smugglers), who made considerable profit from smuggling refugees. It is not that their efforts are not appreciated, it is just that they do not merit consideration for the Righteous Gentile award. In most cases, if the refugee lacked money or other material valuables, then the proffered aid was simply not forthcoming. Only those gentiles who helped Jewish refugees unconditionally are eligible for recognition.

Some recipients of the award did in fact receive money or goods from the Jews which they helped, but were still eligible for the award because the money was given voluntarily and was not a condition for aid. In most cases, the money or other gifts were accepted reluctantly by hosts who were themselves destitute. It must be noted that many of the Righteous Gentiles aided Jews out of their own severe poverty: wartime in an occupied nation is rarely a time of plenty for the honorable.

There are three grades of Righteous Gentile Award. The lowest grade of the award confers a Certificate of Honor printed in both Hebrew and French. The second grade of award confers both the certificate and the right for the recipient to plant a tree by his or her own hand on the Avenue of he Righteous at Yad Vashem in Jerusalem. The highest award confers the certificate and the right to plant a tree at Yad Vashem, and also a gold medal cased in a polished olive wood box.

The right to plant a tree has special significance (see Psalm 1) because it honors friends who did not wither when the world turned hostile toward the Jews. The carob tree is used because, according to Peter Hellmann, "Its glistening and leathery leaves stand up to the [hot] dry winds of summer and the damp winds of winter. They do not wither." Hellman tells us further that Yad Vashem sees Christian significance in the carob because they believe that the "honey" of Mark 1:6 is most properly rendered "carob," a tree which grows in abundance in the Judean wilderness. It is noted that the carob fruit is known traditionally as "Saint John's bread" among Christians in the region.

Some of the Righteous Gentiles suffered much for their compassion for the Jews. When God admonishes us to care for those in trouble, He never promises that the journey will be easy, that there are no hazards. Some of the Righteous were minor officials like Paul Grueninger and Aristedes de Sousa Mendes. Grueninger was a police chief in a small Swiss border town, while Sousa Mendes was a Portuguese consul in France. Both men aided many escaping Jews and lost both their jobs and their civil service pensions for their efforts. Others are like Ona Simaite, the little librarian of Vilna. She could have let the war pass her by, but she did not. Or they are like the little Russian Orthodox nun in Paris, Mother Maria Skbotsova who was executed in the women's camp at Ravensbrueck— some say she volunteered to take the place of a Jewish woman who was selected for the gas chambers. When one of the SS guards from Ravensbrueck was tried for war crimes in 1947, he called her "that wonderful Russian nun," and he averred, "her death was a mistake, we didn't want her to die." We will also meet Pastor André Pascal Trocmé, a French Protestant pastor in a rural village who become one of the spiritual and ethical giants of the Holocaust. None of these people were important or well known before the war, but their inspiring stories are true.

Few of the heroes whose stories are told in this book were heroes in the usual sense of the word. Most were not even part of any organized effort, so could draw little succor or support from like-minded brethren. For the most part, they were ordinary Christians who found themselves in an extraordinary situation that tested their Christian ethics to the very core. It is important to learn from these people what heroism means. It was not that they were unafraid of the consequences of defying the Nazis, but that they overcame that fear and obeyed God despite the wrenching in their guts. According to Peter Hellman in *Avenue of the Righteous,* describing the aid that one Christian woman extended to a Jew: "but *even as she trembled,* she reached out for his arm to bring him into the house."

Let's examine the stories of some of those who, even as they trembled, reached out to bring a Jewish refugee into safety.

3

Guns and Roses: Ona Simaite

When most of the people wailed "What could *I* do?" the Righteous Gentiles proclaimed "What *ELSE* could I do?"

A Jewish poet and survivor of the Vilna ghetto, Abba Kovner, wrote: "If there are only ten Righteous Gentiles among the nations of the world, then Ona Simaite is to be counted among them." Ona was a Lithuanian woman who lived an unextraordinary life before the Germans came to her native land. Ona was a little on the stout side, and was of Eastern European peasant heritage. She had neither the age nor the physique that one expects of soldiers, yet she was very much a soldier in the front lines of the war to save the Jews of Vilna.

Eastern Europe before World War II was deeply mired in virulent anti-Semitism. Centuries of foreign domination and border wars along the Russian-Polish frontier had magnified normal patriotic feelings of nationalism and had made xenophobia a common cancer. The Jews were not just "Christ killers" in a nominally Christian country, but were a foreign element to be despised and, if possible, driven out of the country. For centuries before Hitler, the Jews of the Eastern European Pale of Settlement had lived and died under the most deadly forms of anti-Semitism.

But in Ona Simaite's childhood home, the teaching of her liberal grandfather was that anti-Semitism and all other forms of bigotry were wrong, and that the Jew should be judged each according to his or her own merits. In the Simaite household, Jews were considered human—a novel and unpopular point of view at the time.

During Ona's high school years in Riga, she joined the Socialist Revolutionary Movement, an underground political club that opposed the Czarist monarchy of Russia which then ruled her country. She eventually graduated from the Moscow Teacher's Seminary, and became involved in caring for and educating the children of the poor. When World War II began for Lithuania, Ona Simaite was the head of the cataloging department at the library of the University of Vilna.

Life could have easily passed by Ona Simaite; she could have looked the other way (as did many of her countrymen) when the Germans herded the Jews of Vilna into a ghetto that had been the worst slum of the city. An unnoticed cataloging librarian in an uncontroversial university could have sat out the war with little more than the usual privation. But Ona did not just sit out the war, for she was propelled by "a force much higher than myself."

When the Germans came to Vilna they first forced the Jews to leave their homes and live in the walled-off slum area which became the infamous Vilna Ghetto. By the end of 1941, there were thousands of Jews slowly starving to death in the ghetto.

Ponar Prison was located near the ghetto, and some of the first executions of the Holocaust took place within its walls. The Germans herded 1500 to 2000 Jews at a time into Ponar, and then murdered them with machine-gun fire. Everyone in and out of the ghetto knew that a trip to Ponar was inevitably fatal.

The Nazis also murdered Jews in the forests surrounding Vilna. Groups of Jews would be taken into the woods and forced to dig mass open-pit graves under the pretense of digging anti-tank ditches for defense against the Russians. When the graves were finished, the victims were lined up at the edge of the pit and machine-gunned. A layer of fresh dirt half covering the bodies of the dead was tossed in, and another group would then be brought to the rim and shot.

Such was the terror that was just beginning in Vilna when Ona Simaite began her crusade against the SS.

Imagine the scene in the SS commandant's office. Seated at the desk in the perpetually well-pressed uniform of a full colonel was the commandant of the occupying SS regiment, a man who held the power of life and death over everyone in the area—not just the ghetto victims. Standing plaintively in front of the steely-eyed SS officer was this plump little peasant-faced woman from the library prattling some nonsense about him locking up all of those Jews before they returned their now-overdue library books!

It was not common practice among SS commanders to allow non-Jews into and out of a ghetto, but in this case, the SS commander relented and allowed Miss Simaite of the library to carry out her mission to rescue valuable books from those thieving Jews!

Perhaps it was amused cynicism that spoke to him, or perhaps he wanted to rid himself of this tiresome librarian who had insinuated herself into his life. Whatever the reasons, Ona Simaite received permission from the boss SS man to go into the Vilna Ghetto to retrieve "overdue library books."

For several weeks Ona was able to go into the ghetto at will. After the Germans complained that her mission was taking too long, she invented other ruses to continue her trips in and out of the walled-off area. All together, Ona spent several months as a courier between the ghetto and the outside world. She smuggled in guns, food, medicines and even a bouquet of roses for women who thought they had seen the last of anything beautiful. If she had been caught with *any* of that contraband, she would have been summarily shot.

Ona also smuggled contraband out of the ghetto: diaries, letters, archives, scrolls of the Law, rare Jewish books and other precious objects that would be able to speak to later peoples of the horrors suffered by the previous owners who went through a Time of Jacob's Trouble. The archival materials smuggled out by Ona Simaite were hidden from the Germans in the vaults of the Institute of Linguistics at the University of Vilna.

As early as 1942 the Gestapo was suspicious of Ona. Jacob Gens, Jewish leader of the ghetto, had warned her that the Germans were suspicious of her activities. But Ona continued on, and in the months that followed she was responsible for saving many of the ghetto children. By bribing ghetto guards (many of whom were fellow Lithuanians), cajoling her countrymen, and by outright deceit, she hid away many Jewish children in the homes of gentiles. By the end of the war, there were hundreds of Jews whose survival had depended upon this remarkable woman.

Ona Simaite eventually had to go underground to avoid arrest by the Gestapo. She was successful for a while, but in the summer of 1944 the Gestapo caught up with her. She was taken to Gestapo headquarters in Vilna and interrogated in a manner that only the agents of Satan could conceive. Despite torture and beatings she never betrayed any of "her" children, or the Lithuanians who sheltered them. "I prayed," Ona afterwards told one of her children, "that I might give nothing away . . . with all my heart I prayed, and my prayer was answered."

The Gestapo sentenced Ona to death for her activities. The sentence was never carried out, however, because someone from the university bribed a high German official to commute her sentence to life imprisonment in a concentration camp (then nearly equivalent to a death sentence!) Ona was sent first to Dachau Concentration Camp near Munich in Germany, and then to a camp in France.

She was liberated from the camp in France in 1945 by Allied troops. She then lived in nearby Toulouse for a while, penniless and in poor health. She worked with her hands as a dishwasher in a small restaurant, then as a laundress, a seamstress and, finally, in her old occupation as a librarian.

Word spread among the postwar Jewish community that Ona Simaite had severe health and financial problems. By then, "her children" had emigrated to all points of the globe, including both the United States and Israel . . . and they did not forget the saintly little woman whose sacrifices made their survival possible. In the spring of 1953, Ona Simaite was taken to Israel to live. Although she initially refused assistance, she was eventually forced by failing health to accept the lifetime pension offered to her by a grateful Israeli government.

4

The City of Refuge . . .
Where Goodness Happened

"Keep loving each other as brothers. Do not forget to entertain strangers, for by doing so some people have entertained angels without knowing it" (Hebrews 13:1-2).

Most of us will never experience a test of our Christian ethics in any crucible so severe as the Holocaust. But many European Christians were tested and, for most, the fragile edifice of their ethics proved to have a very low melting point. In the little provincial French village of Le Chambon-sur-Lignon, however, things were different: goodness happened there.

Le Chambon is a French Protestant Huguenot village located on the River Lignon in the hill country between Lyon and the Swiss border. The village has been Protestant for centuries, so it had a long history of resistance in Roman Catholic France. When the Jewish refugees started coming to Le Chambon in 1940, they were often secreted in the same hiding places that had once sheltered Protestant pastors and Calvinist refugees in the post-Reformation era.

The main businesses of Le Chambon are farming and tourism. During the winter months when the farms are dormant and the tourists are back in their homes, the village of Le Chambon falls into somnolence to await the return of spring. It was during the fearsome winter of 1940-41 that the Christian ethics of the Chambonaise began the test. That winter was made more bitter than usual by the concurrence of the worst weather in more than a century and France's recent defeat at the hands of the Germans. It was during that winter that the first of many freezing, terrified Jews appeared in the doorway of the Le Chambon presbytery.

Author and ethicist Philip Hallie, in his book *Lest Innocent Blood Be Shed,* called Le Chambon the safest place in all of Nazi-occupied Europe for Jews. The people of that village hid the refugees, gave them aid out of their own profound poverty, and smuggled many hunted people over the border into neutral Switzerland . . . all at the risk of their own lives and the lives of those dearest to them.

What was the motivation of those people? What caused simple villagers to risk death and torture by hiding refugee Jews whom they didn't even know? The answer needs only one word: *Jesus.*

It was the love of Jesus, as expressed by the teaching and living example of Pastor Andre Pascal Trocmé, that galvanized Le Chambon to nonviolent resistance to the German perversion. It was not the corny, vapid "love" preached by unthreatened pastors who can only rail against nonspecific evils from safe pulpits, but a mortally dangerous love pitted against evil incarnate.

Pastor Trocmé was born on Easter Sunday, 1901, in that part of France which hosted World War I. As a very young child he witnessed the horror of war in his own home province, and was thereafter a confirmed pacifist. The Trocmé family had been Huguenots for many generations, and one of their ancestors had been among the original followers of John Calvin.

During the 1920's, when Hitler was just starting his political career in nearby Germany, Andre Trocmé was in New York studying at Union Theological Seminary. He had won a scholarship and used the opportunity to study the much admired "Social Gospel" of that era. To the spiritually minded Trocmé, however, the Social Gospel had become too secularized; to him it was a good idea that went wrong. During his stay in New York, Andre Trocmé earned extra income by tutoring David and Winthrop Rockefeller in French.

Following his return to France, Trocmé and his wife Magda settled into the comfortable if sparse life of the Protestant pastorate. On the eve of World War II, Trocmé answered the call to the pulpit at the village of Le Chambon.

The new pastor in Le Chambon proved to be a dynamic leader. He was reportedly a "people person" who possessed an embarrassingly expressive love for all of God's creatures. His temper was also embarrassingly expressive, but it would evaporate as rapidly as it exploded.

According to Trocmé's own notebooks, the desire of his heart was to "not be separated from Jesus."

Philip Hallie reports that the people of Le Chambon ". . . called him *un unspiré*, a person inspired by his devotion to Jesus to move and to shake the lives of those around him."

The key to Trocmé's personality is perhaps best illustrated by his attitude toward those that he helped. He never made them feel as if they owed him anything, which they did in abundance, but rather, that *he* was grateful to them for allowing him to save their lives. For example, the French historian Jules Isaac noted that Trocmé tried to convince him that it was Isaac who was helping Trocmé, not the other way around.

Shortly after arriving in Le Chambon, Pastor Trocmé strengthened the chain of thirteen home Bible study groups. His teaching method was to instruct the Bible study leaders so that they, in turn, could return to their respective groups to teach the meaning of the chapter or passage under discussion. One indicator of Trocmé's leadership is that existing Bible study groups more than doubled in size after his arrival and came to include large numbers of young people.

Despite the strong Christian leadership in Le Chambon (which also included the directors of both the public and Christian schools in the village), it would be wrong to characterize the rescue efforts as solely the product of the leader's efforts. The entire village was involved in the resistance: the people were the troops in Trocmé's nonviolent war, the home Bible studies were the infantry squads and the Bible study leaders were the squad commanders. It was a community effort that continued unabated even after the three leaders, including Trocmé, were arrested and sent to a concentration camp.

Jewish refugees who came to Le Chambon usually arrived on the afternoon train and then made their way to the Presbytery. Most of them had somehow heard that Pastor Trocmé would help them, but they had no idea what that meant. All they knew was the depth of their own desperation. They arrived destitute and frightened and had nothing to offer in exchange for their lives . . . except gratitude. Unlike other *passeurs* along the Franco-Swiss border, the Chambonaise asked for nothing: the coin of gratitude and the knowledge that they were obeying God was payment enough.

The refugees were handed over to one of the thirteen Bible study leaders, and from there went to a place of hiding or escape. Those who did not look too ethnically Jewish often lived in the open in Le Chambon, while others led a more secretive life in a house of refuge or on one of the surrounding farms. Some of the Jews, especially later in the occupation, were smuggled into neutral Switzerland. It is not known how many Jews survived the Holocaust because of the Chambonaise, but it is known that the population of Le Chambon was swollen considerably over pre-war levels.

The love and compassion of the people was contagious enough to make allies in the strangest places. Even elements of the notorious Vichy Police, who collaborated with the Germans in almost every other matter, aided the rescue effort. That there were friends in the Police Administration is shown by the warnings received by Trocmé of impending raids. Only once or twice during the entire occupation did these friends fail to warn the pastor of an upcoming raid. Usually, the warning came at night on the telephone: "Tomorrow! Tomorrow!" the mysterious caller would whisper. Pastor Trocmé then alerted the thirteen Bible study leaders, who, in turn, sent their own people or the Boy Scouts to warn those in hiding. By morning there were no Jews in any of the houses or farms. The Vichy Police and the Gestapo came and found no one to arrest.

That God placed friends in critical places is also witnessed by the matter of the *Kennkartes* (identification cards). Everyone in all of the occupied countries needed an I.D. card, or *Kennkarte,* and it was a serious crime to be caught without one. The cards were crucial not just to a avoid arrest, but also to buy rations. A person who lacked a *Kennkarte* was indeed in dire straits. To complicate matters, the security-conscious Germans changed the *Kennkartes* frequently. The people were given only a short time to obtain their new cards before the old cards expired. By this trick, the Nazis were able to flush out many refugees . . . the manufacture of new counterfeit cards took time!

In Le Chambon there is still a mystery concerning the *Kennkartes.* Someone in the police administration, the only source of legitimate cards, apparently kept Pastor Trocmé supplied with blank cards. Whenever the supply of blanks dropped to one or two, or whenever a new card was about to be issued, the mysterious friend supplied a new batch to the pastor. The Trocmé's would open their back door early one morning and find a small stack of blank cards left on the doorpost sometime in the night . . . with no indication of who supplied them. The Jews of Le Chambon did not have to rely on dangerous counterfeit cards, for they had the genuine article. There are those who suppose that it was an angel who supplied those life-saving bits of cardboard!

Jispa

Doing God's work never carries any guarantee of easy passage. In fact, it is often the case that those who answer the call must work the hardest and give up the most; such was true of the Trocmé family. The presbytery was not just the gateway to Trocmé's deuteronomical "City of Refuge," but its nerve center as well. People came and went at all hours, and some of them were residents of the house. No one in Le Chambon bore a heavier load than Magda Trocmé, the pastor's wife. By the winter of 1942-43, after two years of resistance, the overworked Magda was on the edge of desperation and in failing health. Fortunately, God has a way of seeing our needs even before we ourselves see them. Even before Magda Trocmé was ready to cry for outside help, God was setting the stage to provide for her. There was a Protestant community in the city of Avignon whose people were deeply religious. According to some accounts they were French pentecostals, while others call them separated fundamentalists (both could be correct, as the group may have been pentecostals living in a commune together, or a separated community like the Amish in the U.S.). When the community heard of Magda Trocmé's need, they volunteered to send one of their female members to assist with the housekeeping and child-rearing chores. At first, the independent Magda was reluctant to accept their offer, despite her own condition, because the Protestants in Avignon were deeply committed to a total religious life-style that included prayer several times a day and incessant Bible reading. To the more worldly Magda, their ways seemed intimidating. Magda put off accepting their offer of help until January, 1943. By that time, she was on the verge of sheer helplessness and the offered help seemed a lot less intimidating because of her own dire need.

Not long after Magda decided to accept the help offered by the Avignon community, a happy, round-faced little woman named Alice Reynier appeared at the presbytery in Le Chambon. She asked that everyone call her "Jispa," an acronym made up from the initial letters of the French words for "Joy Is Serving in Peace and Love." Jispa came to spend only a few months but stayed more than three decades.

Before Jispa came to Le Chambon she found herself even more intimidated by the move than Magda Trocmé! The reputation of Pastor Trocmé had spread throughout the region, and he was widely regarded as one of the most important Protestant leaders in all of France. Although Trocmé himself would probably have been appalled at the title, he was widely regarded as a spiritual giant. When Jispa heard that she was selected to serve the Trocmé family as a maid, and could thereby share in God's work in Le Chambon, she fell to her knees and thanked God for the opportunity.

It was not long after Jispa's arrival that she became a crucial member of the Trocmé household.

She became an important contributor to the work of saving the Jews. Besides her household chores, Jispa also distinguished herself as a counterfeiter of signatures on forged documents, a job that Trocmé loathed. The arrival of the energetic Jispa freed Magda to share more in the work of her husband. Where Andre Trocmé was the spiritual and political head of the village refugee effort, Magda was the mover who made things happen.

Trocmé's Ethics

Ethics is a study that can be safely overlooked by many of us, especially those Christians who ordinarily lead righteous lives without overt sin. Some of us even succumb to situation ethics and try to make it look Christian. But when the issue is life and death, as it was during the Holocaust, the significance of our decisions is so tremendous that we can no longer overlook the matter. The direction those decisions will take depends in large measure on motivation. For Trocmé, the most basic ethical issue was simply obedience to God's will. In the words of Hallie: "His obedience to Jesus was not like the obedience of a soldier to a military leader; it was more like the obedience of a lover to his beloved. He wanted to be close to Jesus, a loving disciple who put his feet in Jesus' footprints with stubborn devotion."

Issues are complex in situations like the Holocaust, and that complexity often translates into inaction and lost lives. Energy that could be spent aiding the victims is wasted in heated debate and theoretical discussions. For the Chambonaise, howver, the time for theory was past and the issues were starkly simple:

one either helps, or one does not. To a community of faith, which Christians are called to be, giving aid to a hunted people like the Jews of the Holocaust was merely an act of obedience to God. The practical ethic of the Chambonaise can be rephrased: one either obeys God, or one does not. To the Christian, who lives with the promise of eternal life and the knowledge that all he has including life is God's, the matter of risk to life is not even an admissible consideration if obedience to God requires one to lay down that life.

Pastor Trocmé was unusual in that his obedience to God did not lead to a formal program, nor to a system of methods, nor to an organization in the formal sense of the word. To Trocmé, who often spoke of the "power of the Spirit" to the apparent perplexity of author Hallie, obedience to God meant allowing the Holy Spirit to do His will; ". . . it was a surprising power, a force that no one can predict or control." According to Hallie, Trocmé ". . . himself embodied the surprising force he spoke about so often." Christians would probably say that he was "filled with the Spirit."

The practical Christianity of Trocmé, a philosophy which he communicated both in his sermons and in his personal life, can be summed up by the Sermon on the Mount, and also by the story of the Good Samaritan. The question prompted by so-called "Second Greatest Commandment," *love your neighbor as you love yourself,* is: "who is my neighbor?" The answer for Trocmé: anyone in dire need. The philosophy which Trocmé personified was that obedience to God's will does not just mean keeping the Ten

Commandments and attending church services, but, in the spirit of the Sermon on the Mount, he held that even passively watching another in an act of harm-doing was in itself an act of harm-doing. Watching the SS man murder a Jew was the same to Trocmé as doing the murder himself!

Trocmé's personal ethics came out in other ways. For example, he refused to evangelize the children of the Jewish refugees. While, in other circumstances, he would have been a passionate evangelist, he regarded it as unethical to evangelize the refugee children entrusted to his care; it was a violation of trust. While many Christians find fault with Trocmé over this issue, he felt that aid given only for the sake of propaganda—even if that propaganda were the Gospel—was not in the spirit of obedience to God. His actions, and those of the Chambonaise, spoke more eloquently of the love of God, the kingship of Jesus and the Gospel than any forced evangelism could hope for.

The Concentration Camp and Flight

Pastor Trocmé did not hide his activities, so he was well known to the Vichy Police. Trocmé believed that even white lies were false witness, and therefore repugnant to God—an act of disobedience to the Commandments. To maintain the security of his network without having to lie meant working without knowing who was sheltering the refugees, or even the names of the refugees being hidden. When the Vichy Police asked for a list of people involved with him he would not deny his own involvement, but he refused to divulge anything that he knew. "I am their pastor, their shepherd. It is not the role of a shepherd to betray the sheep confined to his keep." That ethic cost him a trip to the concentration camp.

The Vichy Police came to Le Chambon during the evening of February 13, 1943. The small raiding party was led by a police major named Silvani. In the manner typical of the Trocmés, they appeared to bear the embarrassed Silvani no ill will. The ever practical Magda even fed dinner to their persecutor while he waited for Andre.

The police arrested schoolmasters Edouard Theiss (director of the Christian school) and Roger Darcissac (director of the public school), in addition to Pastor Trocmé. The three men were marched slowly up the road to the village square where a khaki-colored police van was parked. As they walked, villagers began to fall in along the route to see their leaders off to an unknown fate. As the arrested men neared the van they could hear their flock singing "A Mighty Fortress Is Our God," a musical sentiment that would be tested for them in the very near future. The three men from Le Chambon were sent to the concentration camp at Saint Paul d'Eyjeaux, near the French city of Limoges. All three men were certain that they were going to their deaths, for that was the reputation of the camps by that time!

The villagers of Le Chambon burdened the three prisoners with gifts that had become very precious to the poverty-stricken people during wartime: chocolates, sausage, sardines and a roll of most precious toilet paper—the latter being a most exceptional luxury during those hard times. When Pastor Trocmé arrived in the camp he opened the coveted toilet paper and found that some unknown villager had lovingly penned relevant Bible verses on the outer sheets!

The other inmates of the camp were astonished at the large number of gift packages that arrived regularly for the trio from Le Chambon. The gifts were so numerous that the men had to build shelves over their bunks to store the supplies. At first, the other inmates thought that the men were rich, but they soon came to understand that it was the love of the villagers that caused them to part with such valuable treasures. One battle-hardened leader of a French Communist resistance cell was astonished at Christians who behaved as pure Marxist doctrine claimed that men would live in a perfect society!

God did not want the leaders of Le Chambon to die in Hitler's camps. When the men arrived at the camp they were resigned to live out the short remainder of their lives in concentration camps, far from their beloved people. For some reason that has never been satisfactorily explained, all three men were *suddenly released from custody and sent home!* A few days after some clerical error caused their release, the camp was closed and all the other inmates were transferred to the killer camps of the east; all of them died of either hard work or in the gas chambers of Maidanek in Poland.

Shortly after Trocmé returned home, the German army moved south to occupy the Vichy section of France. The Italians had overthrown Mussolini and surrendered to the Allies, so the German *Wehrmacht* (regular army) had to cover the southern flank recently vacated by the Italian army. With the arrival of the

German army, the Chambonaise were faced with not just the Vichy Police with its Gestapo "advisors," but the dread Gestapo itself and the troops of the *Waffen-SS* (armed SS). The Gestapo was a considerably greater adversary than the Vichy Police, so Pastor Trocmé had to flee Le Chambon and live the life of a refugee for the last ten months of the occupation.

The Gestapo was actively interested in the Trocmé case, and put out wanted bulletins on him. His name was supposedly on a Gestapo execution list. At every railroad station, at every police checkpoint were SS troops, Gestapo and Vichy police who had pictures and a dossier on Trocmé. All police and troops had orders to arrest Trocmé on sight, and to shoot him if he tried to escape.

Several times during his flight, Trocmé found the life of faith tested and proven valid. Once, when taking refuge in the home of a fellow pastor in the town of Lamastre, the Gestapo raided the house only a few hours after he left. The pastor's wife had taken him in without her husband's permission. When the pastor returned home he was aghast that so dangerous a fugitive as Trocmé was in his living room and ordered him to leave immediately. Only a few hours after Trocmé left, the Gestapo raided the house looking for him!

Another episode showed God's protection of the fleeing pastor. Trocmé was waiting in the train station at Lyon for a train to Valence. With him was his twelve-year-old son, Jacot. The pair somehow came to the attention of a German soldier who ordered them at gunpoint to report to a small table where an officer was checking identity papers. The honest Trocmé was travelling on false I.D. papers, but resolved not to lie. He was ready to admit his identity even though it could mean death for himself and possibly Jacot also. Trocmé and his son were in a line with other detainees awaiting examination by the officer at the control point. The German soldier who had arrested them was close at hand, keeping an eye on his captives. Suddenly, Trocmé realized that a stone pillar blocked the view of the German, so he carefully instructed his son Jacot to walk slowly away from the lineup with him. They both disappeared into the train station crowd and, according to one account, were singing hymns in a nearby Protestant church less than fifteen minutes later. The German soldier was rewarded for his diligence with a transfer to the deadly Eastern Front. When Trocmé heard of the German's fate, he prayed that the young soldier would not die under the Russian meatgrinder that was pressing the Germans hard from the east.

God also protected the village from harm during that period. The dread *Waffen-SS Tartar Legion* was stationed about twenty-five kilometers from Le Chambon, yet was never ordered into action against the Chambonaise. The Tartar Legion was a division of Moslem Croates formed into their own SS unit (despite Nazi racial theories!), and were specially trained to make reprisals against villages and towns who offered resistance to the Nazis. The Tartar Legion carried out several *Aktions* against other villages— executing the men and razing the houses—but never came to Le Chambon.

The only casualties in Le Chambon were Trocmé

cousin Daniel Trocmé and some of the refugee children who were in Daniel's care. In the case of Daniel, following the only successful raid on Le Chambon that netted Jewish prisoners, he was sent to the concentration camps in the east. He refused to disavow his assistance to the Jews, much to the consternation of the Germans. After the war, the Trocmé family found out that Daniel was murdered in the gas chambers of Maidanek about two o'clock in the morning April 4, 1944. The Gestapo men who interrogated Daniel so cruelly continued to investigate him after his death. They were never convinced that his stubborn defense of the Jews was the act of a gentile; they believed that he was at least part Jewish and Daniel Trocmé never disabused them of that notion!

5
"That Wonderful Russian Nun . . ."

The Angel of Ravensbrueck: Mother Maria of Paris

The hot July sun pounded down on the tall ruddy-faced Russian nun as she trudged up to one of the French policemen guarding the entrance to Paris' famous sports stadium and race track, the Vel d'Hív. The policeman was more bored than alert, so he gave her papers only a quick look before granting her passage into the stadium.

It was the second day of the infamous week-long roundup of Paris Jews. Adolf Eichmann's notorious representative, Theodore Dannecker, conducted the roundup, and within 24 hours there were nearly 7,000 Jews interned in the stadium. The raids had begun on July 16, 1942, at 4 A.M. and were still going on at 1 P.M. the next day when Mother Maria made her way to the stadium.

Dannecker had originally scheduled the roundup to begin on July 13, but that plan was canceled when it was realized that it meant conducting an *Aktion* on Bastille Day, July 14. The French regard Bastille Day as dearly as Americans do the Fourth of July, and the SS feared a general uprising if they desecrated the French holiday.

The midday brightness stunned Maria as she emerged from the dark pedestrian tunnel that led into the stadium's inner ground. The scene that met her eyes as they adjusted to the light was like none seen in France since the Middle Ages. Thousands of Jews, about half of them children, were corralled together like cattle with no accommodations, food or water.

Dannecker's SS had been brutally efficient, even though his eventual toll would be 15,000 fewer than his orders demanded. Seriously ill Jewish patients taken from their hospital beds lay alongside whole families who were arrested while eating dinner. Prisoners with infectious diseases were not treated, and were merely quarantined by quartering them in the once high-cost boxes reserved by the wealthy to watch horse races.

The French Boy Scouts arrived to provide water for the prisoners. Municipal water had been turned off, and it delighted the SS sense of humor to keep it turned off except for a bare trickle. Sturdy adolescent backs bent under the repeated burden of water pails. But despite the heroic efforts of the scouts there was not nearly enough water in the stadium for all the thousands of internees.

Food was also in short supply in the Vel d'Hív. Except for a few bundles brought by the well-prepared, the only food was inadequate supplies of soup provided by the French Red Cross. "What did Jews need of precious food supplies?" reasoned the SS bureaucrats. Hitler's Final Solution was already a year old, and several of a hideous new form of concentration camp—death camps—had been operating in Eastern Europe for six months. Auschwitz was only a three-day train ride away, so what need did Jews have for food?

Maria soon found the object of her quest. A Jewish woman whom she had known at the Russian Orthodox convent on Rue de Lourmel had been arrested and taken to the stadium along with her four children. Madame G. was almost hysterical with delight when she spotted the familiar nun. Maria was especially welcomed for the bread, sausage and cheese concealed beneath her robes.

All during the afternoon and evening Maria comforted Madame G. and the four children huddled around her. After the woman and four children fell asleep, Maria went to work assisting the bone-weary nurses and the two Jewish doctors who staffed the Red Cross hospital that had been hastily set up in the stadium. Mother Maria once again exhibited her utter disdain for both personal comfort and rest. Like many times before, she worked around the clock oblivious to her own need for food or sleep.

On the morning of the second of her three days in Vel d'Hív, Maria hit upon an idea for saving the four children of her friend. Nazi bureaucrats who refused to send in water and food supplies were concerned about *litter* in the stadium! A crew of French trashmen were sent in everyday with their horse-drawn trash carts to remove refuse. Maria quickly made friends with the trash foreman, whom she pressed into service more by the force of her personality than anything else. She scribbled an address on a scrap of paper and then pressed it into the unwilling hands of the foreman, who pocketed it without reading it.

One by one she smuggled the children to the trash bins under her robes, and dumped them in like so much litter. If the French police saw her, they turned and looked the other way; fortunately, no informers or Germans saw the proceedings.

The children of Madame G. were removed from the stadium and survived the Holocaust. Their mother was deported to Auschwitz the next day, where she died.

Just hours before the doomed of Vel d'Hív were transferred to the death camp, the Germans forced all non-Jews to leave the stadium. "All Jew-lovers get out!" bellowed the SS Inspector, who ordered her to leave. Mother Maria was too exhausted to protest—she had been working without rest for more than three long, hot July days.

To understand Mother Maria's simple heroism during the Holocaust one has to examine the whole course of her life. It seems that God guided her for decades prior to World War II, shaping a personality that was able to resist the most demonic movement in all of history.

Maria was born in 1891 in Czarist Russia, and was named Elisabeth ("Lisa") Pilenko. Her father, Yuri Pilenko, was a General in the Russian Imperial army who had returned to grow grapes and produce wine in the Black Sea town of Anapa. The Pilenko vineyards prospered when General Pilenko pioneered a method for culturing grapes on the sandy beach.

His Red Cabernet wine won a Gold Medal in the All-Russia Exposition. The family was well-to-do by any standards, and moved among aristocratic circles both in Moscow and the Imperial capital of St. Petersburg. General Pilenko had connections in the Imperial Court itself, a matter of some social and economic consequence for the family.

Lisa's early life was one of privilege and prosperity amid the squalor and hopeless poverty of the Russian masses in the years before the Revolution of 1917. Although she had no first-hand knowledge of privation in those years, her writings reveal a growing social consciousness engendered by an increasing love of God.

Yet beneath the happy, adolescent sparkle of the youthful Lisa, there was a prophetic foreboding. She repeatedly had a vision of death by burning, and dreamed of ". . . companions in my coffin," a fitting preview of the crematoria and mass graves of the Ravensbrueck Concentration Camp where she was to eventually die three decades later.

Despite a brief period of agnosticism following the death of her father in 1906, Lisa nurtured a love of God that grew even during the period of her life when she moved among the elite circles of literary and intellectual figures in St. Petersburg. Lisa and her first husand, Dmitri Kuzmina-Karavaeva, included among their circle of intimates the occultist-philosopher Nicholas Berdyaev, writer Alexei Tolstoi, future Nobel Prize winner Boris Pasternak and the poet Alexander Blok.

The schedule kept by the intellegentsia of St. Petersburg was absurd. They typically slept until late afternoon, seldom rising before 3 P.M. By late evening the youthful troupe would gather at Berdyaev's flat— which was nicknamed "The Tower"—where they would debate all manner of subjects until dawn. Following a traditional breakfast of fried eggs the group would break up for another day.

It was commonplace amongst the intellectuals to scoff at Christianity. Revolution was their nominal religion (although only a few actually participated when it came!), and they talked incessantly about it being the "Third Testament." All of the talk by her atheist and agnostic friends had the opposite of the intended effect on Lisa Pilenko. During that period she drew ever closer to Christ. When World War I shattered their peaceful lives, and sent her friends into bitter confusion over patriotism and revolution, she was able to remark: "I know their only need is Jesus."

During her pre-World War I years in St. Petersburg, Lisa dedicated herself to writing verse, to painting and to theological studies. Her verse was not unrecognized, and she was able to publish two volumes of her poetry. Her poems revealed both a heart yearning for God and an immense love for God's children. Her paintings were almost exclusively icons, a religious art form common in the Orthodox churches.

Lisa's theological studies were done at home under the direction of the faculty of the St. Petersburg Ecclesiastical Academy. Although she was the first woman in history to be admitted to the academy, she was not permitted to attend classes because she was female. Her sponsor kept her supplied with the texts and the official lecture notes, and she finished the course in the same time as the regular students. Despite her brilliant performance on the oral examination, however, she was denied graduation because one of the professors was adamantly opposed to women theology students.

Lisa's first marriage ended in divorce, with Lisa maintaining custody of their daughter Gayana. Her former husband took orders for the Roman Catholic priesthood, and Lisa poured herself into the work of the Social Revolutionary Party. Years later, when Gayana was grown and working in Moscow as secretary to Tolstoi, she delighted in shocking people by claiming to be the child of a Roman Catholic priest and a Russian Orthodox nun—which of course was true, despite the fact that few people believed her!

The Revolution of 1917 overthrew the old Czarist government, and threw the country into turmoil. Lisa's Social Revolutionary Party won fifty-eight percent of the vote in the only free election ever held in Russia. Lenin's Bolshevik Communists refused to accept the election, however, and soon took over the government at gunpoint. Alexander Kerensky, the head of that government, fled into exile. He eventually settled in Paris, where he became a close associate of Lisa Pilenko.

The tide of revolution turned into a civil war that ebbed and flowed across the face of Russia for several years. The "White" armies of the Social Revolutionaries found themselves pitted against the "Red" armies of the communists. Lisa and another woman decided that Moscow and St. Petersburg were no longer safe for them, so they undertook the dangerous journey back to Anapa.

A long-distance rail journey with small children was difficult enough in Russia at that time. But with a viciously contested civil war raging, there were new and unforeseen hazards. It was during this journey that Lisa Pilenko—who would one day win fame as Mother Maria of Paris—demonstrated the right stuff in the face of mortal danger.

The train south was guarded by a contingent of Bolsheviks under the command of an uncouth sailor named Sakharov. While waiting at a station for a train transfer, the group learned of the approach of a Ukrainian White army under the command of a brigand named Petlyura. Sakharov, not wanting the burden of protecting civilians while under attack from Petlyura's force, decided on summary execution. Passengers were marched off behind the station and shot. When Sakharov came to fetch Lisa and her friend, she demanded that a telegram be sent to Moscow so ". . . that Ulanova (i.e., Lenin!) should know what happened to me, and at what station!" The other woman joined in the ruse that was to save their lives: "Don't you know this is Vladimir Illyich's wife? What sort of Bolshevik are you?" Apparently calling her bluff, Sakharov permitted Lisa to write her message: "Tell Ulanova that I am about to be shot . . ." she didn't even have time to write the second line before the uncertain Sakharov relented and turned the party loose to continue their journey.

Lisa Pilenko maintained her composure until she was safely on the southbound train. When safely away from the Bolsheviks, however, she broke down and for hours alternated between hysterical laughter and convulsive sobbing.

The town of Anapa seemed so far from the fighting that it could serve Lisa and her child as a safe haven. The town was far to the south of the capitals, and was little more than a rural seacoast town on the Black Sea. The civil war had caused the fortunes of Anapa to reverse, however, and their previously prosperous lifestyle was in shambles.

The mayor of Anapa and the town council had quit, and municipal services came to a halt. Power in the town rested not in the town council, but in a Bolshevik committee (called a "Soviet") under the direction of a Red named Protapov. Lisa's family had been the leading landowners of the region, and they still commanded respect in Anapa. Their once prosperous estate was in moribund disrepair, and was producing little income for the family. In February 1918, the citizens of Anapa elected Lisa Pilenko Mayor of the town.

Mayor Pilenko enthusiastically accepted her role, and set out to improve the lot of the people of Anapa and the refugees who poured into the region ahead of the fighting front. She arranged food, shelter and medical treatment for the needy. There was a seedy sanatorium on the outskirts of Anapa which had been under government control for some time before. The doctor who previously owned the institution had a reputation more for greed than for his curative powers, and was a bitter enemy of the Pilenko family. Doctor Budzinsky had been mayor before Lisa and bore much hatred for her. This hatred was only exacerbated when Lisa took over the sanatorium to house refugees.

The bad feeling between Lisa and Budzinsky could have cost her life. When the White Army approached Anapa, the local Bolsheviks disappeared and the local Soviet disbanded. Mayor Lisa Pilenko became the only government in the town.

Lisa had cooperated with the Reds, even though the relationship was stormy and personally dangerous for her. In other towns where the Soviet leader was stronger, Lisa, the Social Revolutionary Party Mayor of the town, would surely have been shot! Yet when the Whites took over Anapa they tossed her into her own jail to await trial for treason. Once again, Lisa Pilenko had good reason to fear a firing squad.

The townspeople who had known her all of her life, and who had benefitted so much from the work of Lisa Pilenko and her father before her, fell strangely silent over her imprisonment. Gratitude is sometimes but a token coin, while fear is most often legal tender.

The chief witness against Lisa was none other than the hate-filled Dr. Budzinsky. The prosecutor Yegorov pressed a venom-filled case against the woman who had only recently been the mayor of a Bolshevik-occupied town.

The President of the Tribunal was a bespectacled thirty-two-year-old schoolmaster named Danilo Skobtsov. It was immediately apparent that Judge Skobtsov was well disposed toward Lisa and contemptuous of her tormenters. He abruptly cut off the proceedings and announced that she was free to go.

There was an immediate attraction between Lisa Pilenko and Danilo Skobtsov. Within a few days they married, and Lisa became Madame Skobtsov.

The fortunes of war turned against the Whites, so it soon became necessary for Lisa and Danilo to flee. As the Communist armies surged south into the Crimea, the family, including the child Gayana and Lisa's mother Sophia Pilenko, fled to the town of Tifliss in Georgia. Lisa was by this time pregnant with her second child. They set sail from Novorossiysk in an elderly Italian steamer that had been resurrected especially for the refugee trade.

The Skobtsovs were among the last to obtain tickets, so they were consigned to the lowest hold in the ship. Thousands of refugees were packed into the stinking, rat-infested space along with a cargo of aluminum. Conditions were so crowded that movement was dangerous. Spaces in the deck planking made a broken leg likely for anyone who dared move about in the dark, fetid hold.

Georgia was not the idyllic place that they had imagined because refugees by the thousand poured into the province. Danilo decided to push on to Constantinople (present-day Istanbul) in Turkey. Constantinople was hospitable towards the refugees, but lacked the capacity to absorb the seemingly endless stream of refugees that poured in from Russia. As a result, the Russian emigrés eventually made their way to Yugoslavia, Bulgaria, the United States or France; the Skobtsov family settled in Paris.

Life for the 45,000 Russian emigrés who settled in Paris after the civil war was hard and cruel. There was too little work, too few opportunities. The dole (welfare) provided money for drink, so alcoholism was rampant. During this period, the once wealthy Lisa Pilenko-Skobtsov earned a mere fifteen francs a day sewing.

Despite their poverty, the Skobtsovs enjoyed the company of the exile intelligentsia and political figures from their homeland. At various times, their circle of friends included Alexander Kerensky (Russia's only non-Soviet elected President), Boris Pasternak (Nobel Prize-winning novelist) and other luminaries of Russian culture. Among the circle was Metropolitan (i.e., Orthodox Bishop) Georgiyevski Evlogy. The bishop was the spiritual head of the Russian community in Paris, and it was to him that the people turned in their despair. In Lisa, the bishop found a willing and devoted social worker. After Danilo qualified as a taxicab driver, the economic fortunes of the family improved, and Lisa found more time for her work among the people. She became part social worker, part evangelist and part Mother Confessor to the down and out among the exile Russians.

Mother Maria (nee Lisa Pilenko) once remarked that each age of her life brought a different "transfixing sorrow." By the mid-twenties the Skobtsovs had three children: Gayana, a son Yuri and a second daughter Nastia. The transfixing sorrow of that era of her life was Nastia's death from meningitis. It was an event that was to impel Maria into ever greater social work, and probably led to the breakdown of her second marriage.

Lisa Pilenko-Skobtsov was introduced to the

Russian Christian Student Movement, an organization that is still in existence today. She worked among the refuse of society: the alcoholic, the criminal, the depressed and the insane.

By 1930, however, exile life had taken its toll on the Skobtsov family; Lisa and Danilo broke up. Metropolitan Evlogy granted them an ecclesiastical divorce, but they never did receive a civil divorce from the French authorities.

Following the dissolution of her marriage Lisa succumbed to the pleas of Evlogy to enter the monastic life of a nun. She was consecrated in March 1932, at the Church of St. Sergei in Paris. Metropolitan Evlogy gave her the canonical name "Maria."

The monasticism of Mother Maria perplexed the aged Evlogy. She was unable to adapt to the contemplative life that is normally expected of a nun, and preferred instead a "new monasticism" which she liked to call "secular monasticism." Her idea was to carry Christ to the downtrodden masses. To her friend, writer Marc Vishniak, she explained, "I would like to become mother to all the poor things of the earth." Maria worked with the conviction that the key to the loneliness and suffering of the exile community was rooted in a loss of faith. Like Pastor Trocmé to the south of her, Mother Maria believed that compassion without action is a debased currency, and evangelism lacking social concern a counterfeit coin.

For her work, Mother Maria was both praised and criticized by a community which failed to realize the depth of her commitment to Christ. When Maria penned "Take me, I am your stone, build with me, inscrutable Architect," she was committing herself to take up a cross for the poor of spirit.

The new movement created by Mother Maria was named "Orthodox Action." It never numbered more than a few ecclesiastics and laymen, and often consisted solely of Maria, her mother Sophia, and her son Yuri.

The compassionate evangelist Maria took the Gospel messages into the places that other missionaries shunned. She carried Christ into the bars and brothels of Marseilles—much to the consternation of "proper" churchmen who preferred a more dignified ministry. But there were many emigrés in that city who needed ministry, and Mother Maria became their only link with the church.

There were also many Russians working for slave-like wages in the mines in the Pyrenees Mountains of southern France. Maria was drawn like a moth to the flame of suffering, but at first she was not well received. "If you want to help," sneered one of the larger emigré workmen, "don't bring us talk, bring us clean floors instead!" The miners' quarters were filthy and unhealthy, and that environment exacted a fearsome spiritual toll from the men. Maria's response was to grab bucket and brush and then get down on her knees to scrub the grimy floors. Contemptuous workmen gathered around to watch this daughter of the landed gentry humbly washing their barracks floor. Maria turned suddenly to renew her water-soaked scrub brush, only to knock over the pail of filthy water and send herself sprawling comically across the floor. The humiliating incident broke the ice with the workmen, and they then allowed her to hold her lecture.

Why God would permit one so dedicated to His service to suffer such humiliation in her ministry we may never know. But there are sometimes hints. As Mother Maria was leaving the mining camp, one of the workers came running after her. He confessed that her coming had postponed—but not canceled—his plans for suicide. Mother Maria insisted that he leave the mines at once and accompany her to the city of Toulouse. She forcibly helped him pack his bags and tugged him to the train station. She left the potential suicide with a family of her acquaintance in Toulouse, where he eventually recovered his mental state.

The convent which Maria founded at 77 Rue de Lournel was like no other in Paris. The neighborhood is close to the Seine, and consists mostly of factories and low-cost apartment houses. The eighteen-room former mansion was too dilapidated to interest anyone else, but to Mother Maria it was a gift from heaven.

There was no work that Maria would not undertake. She gloried in doing the carpentry, cleaning, and decorating, yet at the same time found the time to paint icons and type essays. She despised what she called "white-hands ministry," and under her efforts the convent of Orthodox Action came to life. Although there were many spacious rooms in the house, Maria chose for herself the little cell beneath the stairs.

Ministry at the convent took the form of the kind of social work that Maria was used to for so many years. Maria herself labored longer and harder than any of the others. The ordinary laws of nature had no power over the nun, or so it seemed to those who marveled over her ability to work for days at a time without either food or water.

Her critics lamented her stained and torn robe, and the down-at-the-heel castoff men's shoes that she habitually wore. To Mother Maria, however, such niceties mattered little compared with her need to bring Christ to the destitute. To Maria, one was either ". . . a Christian with fire, or one is not a Christian at all." She scorned the easy life, and contemptuously scolded her critics that it is better to be ". . . God's fool than to sit and drink tea and eat 'Holy Bread.' " When the critics retorted that she set a bad example as a nun, and didn't even attend daily Mass regularly, she responded: "at the Last Judgement the Lord will not ask whether I satisfactorily practiced asceticism, or how many bows I made before the altar. He will ask if I fed the hungry, clothed the sick, visited the sick and prisoners . . ."

The work of the convent proceeded with Maria at the center of a whirlwind. There was a low-cost canteen that fed hundreds of out-of-work emigrés and Parisians daily, a workroom where women earned small amounts sewing, and the ever present compassion of the bone-weary Mother Maria. When the war came, it was natural that 77 Rue de Lourmel became a center of passive resistance to German persecution of the Jews.

To the convent came frightened Jews fleeing the Nazis. Some were hidden at the convent, while others were concealed in the homes of others. Hundreds were passed on to Father Chaillet's Roman Catholic underground organization. From the Catholics, Maria obtained false papers for her Jewish charges

(Father Chaillet had a printing press that turned out counterfeit documents).

The work of the convent was every bit as dangerous as that of the armed resistance. To the Nazis, it didn't matter whether you opposed them with a submachine gun or compassion—the penalty was the same: death or the concentration camp.

Maria's work came to its end in a concentration camp. But the beginning of the end came at midday on Monday, February 7, 1943. The convent was raided by a Gestapo party under the command of an SS-Security Police (SS-SD) Inspector named Hoffman. They came to arrest Mother Maria for her work helping Jews, but, finding that she was not at home, arrested her son Yuri as a hostage.

When Maria returned to the Lourmel convent and heard the news, she hurried to Gestapo headquarters on Avenue Foch. She was promptly arrested and subjected to torture and cruel interrogation.

The next day, February 8, Hoffman summoned Sophia Pilenko (Maria's 80-year-old mother) and Father Dmitri Klepinin (the convent's spiritual leader and Maria's confessor). A summons to Gestapo headquarters was a fearsome thing, and often caused people to go underground, or, in some cases, to die of a heart attack. The elderly Sophia inquired of the priest: "Father Dmitri, what will we tell them?" He opened his ever present Bible at random and found Luke 12:11:

> And when they bring you before the synagogues and the rulers and the authorities, do not become anxious about how or what

you should speak in your defense, or what you should say; for the Holy Spirit will teach you in that very hour what you ought to say.

Herr Hoffman interrogated Sophia first, but could get nothing from her. Father Dmitri was dealt with second, but to Hoffman's surprise he did not deny any of the allegations. He thereby sealed his own fate—he was sentenced to a concentration camp.

Maria realized the danger to the others at Lourmel, so she confessed to the charges without compromising those whom she had helped. The brutal Hoffman scolded Madame Sophia: "You have brought up your daughter badly—she helps only Jews!" To which the elderly Sophia retorted: "That's not true! For her there is neither Greek nor Jew . . . she's a Christian, she would even help you if you needed it!"

Hoffman tried to get the trio to implicate others, but without success. He was suspicious of Dmitri's sister Tanya, who was said to be a member of the resistance. Fortunately, Tanya was warned and escaped the city with her child Andre—who is now known as ballet star Andre Prokovsky.

Mother Maria, Father Dmitri and Yuri Skobtsov were sentenced to the concentration camps, despite Hoffman's early promise to release Yuri. The three were sent first to the camp at Romainville (France). Yuri and Father Dmitri were transferred to the camp at Compiegne on April 21, 1943, while Maria was sent to the women's camp at Ravensbrueck in Germany.

Dmitri and Yuri stayed at Compiegne until January, 1944, when they were transferred to the notorious

Buchenwald camp in Germany. Within a month they were again transferred: they were sent to the much feared subcamp at Dora. This "camp" was no camp at all, but an underground work site. The Germans employed the prisoners digging a pair of tunnels into the Harz Mountains to house a V1 missile installation. Over 5,000 men worked and lived together in the dark, foul tunnels. On February 11, 1944, Father Dmitri succumbed to the cruel conditions; his body was returned to Buchenwald for cremation.

Yuri had contracted a contagious disease called ferunculosis, and could not work. He was last seen a few days after Dmitri's death, climbing into a transport. It is assumed that he was shot.

Maria arrived at Ravensbrueck in April 1943. The train carrying Maria and hundreds of others stopped after a three-day journey at Fuerstenberg Station in the nearby German town of Mecklenburg. The prisoners had been given no water or food, and were packed into cattle cars so tightly that they couldn't move.

To the outsider, there was something almost appealing about the Ravensbrueck Concentration Camp. Adjoining the entrance square on the left was a well-kept white barracks building and an aviary where peacocks were kept. On the other side of the square was a luxurious manicured lawn lined with silver fir trees.

When Ravensbrueck opened in 1940 it was designed to hold 4,000 prisoners in 16 barracks blocks. By 1943, when Maria arrived, the number of barracks blocks had doubled while the inmate population quadrupled to more than 16,000. Each hut held 400 to 800 prisoners, two to four times the number designed for.

The entrance ritual called for the women to strip naked and shower. They were allowed to keep only a small handkerchief and comb, but Maria somehow managed to also retain her pocket New Testament.

The coarse dresses that served as prison uniforms each had a colored cloth that classified the prisoner: red—political, black—"asocials," violet—Jehovah's Witnesses, green—common criminals, pink—homosexuals, yellow—Jews. The Jews sometimes had a second triangle added to the first, inverted to form a Magen David (Star of David). A few Jews had a black border around the star that singled them out for especially brutal treatment. These were the so-called "race defilers," i.e., Jews who were married to gentiles. Those prisoners of whatever category who were suspected of plotting an escape attempt were given an unsubtle warning: a red-and-white target bull's-eye was painted on the back of their uniforms. Being a political prisoner from France, Mother Maria was issued a red triangle with an "F" printed inside.

The peaceful-looking entranceway to Ravensbrueck concealed the extreme brutality within. The women SS guards and their male counterparts of the SS Death's Head Formation had literal power of life and death over the inmates. The slightest infraction, or no reason at all, could bring a flogging, the slap of a rubber truncheon, or the smashing of a rifle butt against the skull. The guards had trained attack dogs that could tear at calves and legs, or if the offense were great enough, the dog would be ordered to disembowel the victim. Volleys of rifle shots were often heard outside the camp. Word would soon go around about another group of undesirables being executed.

Like Mengeler's infamous hospital at Auschwitz, the hospital at Ravensbrueck conducted obscene medical experiments on inmates. SS doctors Gebhard and Rosenthal were hanged after the war for their hellish work in the Ravensbrueck hospital.

And then there were the chimneys of the two crematoria. Perpertually billowing thick clouds of black smoke, the chimneys glowed red at night and frequently belched a flame fifteen feet high. There was no doubt about the crematoria's function, for a sickly sweet pall stung the nostrils of all within several miles of the camp.

Ravensbrueck was not designed as an extermination camp, so it lacked permanent killing machinery. The SS compensated for that oversight by providing mobile gas chambers.

Food rations at Ravensbrueck consisted of a thin meatless soup twice a day and a small scrap of stale or moldy coarse bread. Food parcels from relatives were usually stolen by the SS before they reached the prisoners.

That bare ration was supposed to provide sustenance to work in the several factories of Ravensbrueck or for manual labor out of doors.

In charge of each hut was a prisoner called a Block Senior. These officials could beat and terrorize prisoners at will or put them on report for punishment, and they controlled the food. Maria's Block Senior was a vulgar and brutal woman who was feared by everyone in the barracks. Nevertheless, Maria won her over and managed to squeeze a few concessions from her for the other prisoners.

Maria moved with godly ease through the hellish ground called Ravensbrueck. She uplifted the other prisoners with words of encouragement, Scripture reading and constant prayer. She cared for the sick, shared her own meager food with weaker prisoners and radiated hope for survival. The "wonderful Russian nun," as SS guards came to call her, conducted Bible study classes in the camp. She was especially interested in the Russian female prisoners of war. These women had grown up under the atheist communist government, so they had never heard the Gospel. Maria read to them from her Russian language New Testament, and for most it was the first time they had ever heard the Word.

Several stories are told concerning Mother Maria's death, but though they differ, all may be facets of the same truth. The only fact known for sure is that she died on March 31, 1945, only five weeks before Ravensbrueck was liberated; it was on the Saturday between Good Friday and Easter Sunday.

During the postwar trials of SS guards from Ravensbrueck, many of them expressed fondness for Maria and claimed that her death was a mistake. None of them knew exactly how it happened. Maria should have survived because she possessed an "aryan" I.D. card; she was almost immune from selection for the gas chambers. Even in March 1945, there were still plenty of Jewish women to fuel the death engine.

In late 1944, supplies for the camp were even more scarce than before, so the SS added a savage new wrinkle to the torments heaped on the prisoners. Those who were too old or sick for hard work were sent to a satellite camp called the Youth Camp (*Jugendslager*), formerly a camp for delinquent youth. Rations in the Youth Camp were a mere fraction of the already meager rations of the main camp. The stories conflict concerning how Maria was selected for the Youth Camp. Some claim that she was selected because she was too weak for continued work. Others claim that Maria volunteered for the Youth Camp so that she could bring hope to the hopeless.

Two months in the Youth Camp took a terrible toll on Maria. When her friend Ina Webster saw her on her return to the main camp she was shocked and dismayed. Harsh conditions coupled with one sixth the ration had reduced Maria to a walking skeleton. Still, she was lucky compared with many others in the Youth Camp. Conditions were so malignant that the women dropped like flies. Somehow, that indomitable spirit survived to return to the main camp months later.

She survived the Youth Camp, but her body was broken, her strength was gone. But despite her condition, Maria had one more charity to give. A Jewish woman was selected for the gas chambers. Maria gave away her life-saving aryan I.D. card and took her place. Too weak from her holy work to walk on her own, Mother Maria had to be carried to her execution by SS guards.

Another witness claimed that Maria herself was selected for the gas chamber. Still another witness believes that both stories are true and represent two different selections. In the first, Maria was not selected but voluntarily switched places with a Jewish woman. Thus she was returned to the Youth Camp which was by then being used as a holding facility for the condemned. It was the following day, Good Friday, 1945, that Mother Maria was selected to die.

True to her youthful vision, Maria's death brought her to the fire of the crematoria. Her ashes were heaped with those of the other victims—she finally found her "companions in my coffin."

6

Miracle in Denmark:
The Night the Jews Disappeared

The first Ground Observer station along the German-Danish frontier reported hearing aircraft engine noises at 3:00 A.M. on April 9, 1940. One hour later, a second phone call to General Staff Headquarters in Copenhagen confirmed that German troops were pouring across the border at Krusaa. Reports came in that German soldiers disembarked at Korsoer. By 6:00 A.M., the Danish government had capitulated and 900 years of Danish independence ended.

The German pretext for invading Denmark was prevention of a British invasion, but a more likely reason is that Germany needed Denmark's agricultural capacity to feed the war effort. Danish farms are among the most efficient in all of Europe, and the German war machine requried their productive ability.

Danish resistance to the German invasion was minimal. For a short while, Danish marines held off the Germans at a Navy base while the fleet executed a "scuttle or escape" order. But when the ships were either sunk or had sailed, the machine-gun chatter ceased and the defenders surrendered to the Germans.

Norwegian resistance to the German invasion was considerably different. Heavy coastal guns guarding Oslo inflicted heavy damage on the German navy, so heavy in fact that Hitler had to postpone his plan to invade England later that year. The German battleship *Koenigsburg* suffered such severe damage that it was taken out of service for months while repairs were made.

There have been ill feelings between the Norwegians and the Danes over the lack of Danish resistance against the Nazis (there was no substantial Danish resistance until 1943). The Danish response, however, is understandable when one compares the situations in the two countries. Norway has a large amount of territory compared with tiny Denmark. Much of its terrain consists of forested mountains that provide friendly cover for partisan fighters. In addition, there is a long coastline with hundreds of inlets and secluded beaches where friendly overseas countries could land material, saboteurs and other aid for the underground. Denmark, on the other hand, is small and therefore easily occupied. A relatively small force of tank and air forces backed by infantry was able to subdue the open, flat nation of Denmark in only a short while. In addition, Denmark shares a common border with Germany behind which the enemy forces were able to muster with little fear of detection. The Danes opted for passive resistance, and the scheme worked for about three years.

Hitler declared that Denmark was not an occupied nation at all, but rather a Model Protectorate (*Musterprotektorat*). Under that status, the Danes were allowed to retain at least the outer trappings of freedom. King Christian X remained on the throne and the Danish Parliament still sat even though under German supervision. All seemed normal under the occupation, except for the German presence.

The Germans had determined early in the occupation that the Danes would not tolerate anti-Jewish measures which had been successful in other countries. The Danes had a centuries-old tradition of accepting the Jews, coupled with a habit of rebuking anti-Semites. When the Danes resisted early anti-Semitic overtures by the Germans, the Nazi occupiers decided to shelve the measures until later.

Life continued somewhat normally in Denmark until mid-1943. The Germans restrained themselves from the sort of barbarity that characterized their rule in other countries. But hardships occasioned by the war began to make the population more restless as time went on. The year 1943 was a turning point in World War II because German armed forces experienced the first of several major setbacks. Rommel's string of sudden, spectacular victories ended with the crushing of his vaunted *Afrika Korp* at El Alamein, the Allies invaded the underbelly of Europe by landing in Sicily, and Mussolini was overthrown. The most crushing defeat was the surrender of a massive German army at Stalingrad in Russia.

Suddenly, the Germans didn't look quite so invincible, and that perception gave rise to an increasing

incidence of resistance activity all over Europe—
including Denmark.

By 1943, the Final Solution of the Jewish Problem
(Hitler's euphemism for the extermination of the Jews)
was two years old and millions of victims were already
dead. The death camps operated at full efficiency
around the clock, killing tens of thousands of Jews
each day. But the Danish Jews were still free of
persecution and were able to come and go as they
pleased. Hitler viewed the Jews' freedom in Denmark
as "loathsome," so he summoned *Reichsplenipotentiary*
Dr. Werner Best to Berlin for what might be called a
"wall-to-wall conference." The encounter with Hitler
left Dr. Best "shaken and pale." Best was demoted in
importance, if not actual rank, and *Wehrmacht* (army)
commander in Denmark General von Hannecker was
made head of the occupation government.

The Danish situation continued to deteriorate
throughout August 1943. A pretext for the deportations
presented itself in the form of shipyard workers' strikes
in Copenhagen and Odense. A Danish SS division was
returned from the eastern front to put down the strike
and keep order. Plans were then made for the arrest of
the nation's Jews.

Dr. Best, perhaps attempting to get back in the good
graces of the top Nazi leadership, sent a telegram to
Berlin on September 8, 1943, outlining a plan for the
arrest and deportation of the Jews. The plan called for
a contingent of SS to make the arrests, while
transportation authorities within the German embassy
would make arrangements for the trucks and ships
needed to remove the Jews from Denmark to the

Theresienstadt Concentration Camp. Therein lay a weakness in the German plan: not all members of the German diplomatic service were ardent Nazis. The official in charge of shipping was Georg Ferdinand Duckwitz, a man of conscience.

Dr. Best informed Duckwitz of the plan on September 11, 1943, when he ordered the official to prepare an estimate of shipping needs for the deportation operation. A violent argument ensued between the two men, and Duckwitz stated that he would sooner quit his post than participate in the deportation or persecution of the Jews. Best replied that he too looked with displeasure on the operation, but affirmed that "one must obey orders."

At this late date it may be a little difficult to assess Dr. Best's intentions, but a day or so later there occurred a conversation between Best and Duckwitz that almost seems like Best was inviting Duckwitz to warn the Danes of the impending raid. Whatever the stimulus, however, it is known that Duckwitz did in fact tip off the Danes.

Before acting, however, Duckwitz had to confirm the truth of Best's statements. He flew to Berlin on September 13 and made certain discreet inquiries in the Foreign Ministry. He was told that Best's plan was accepted, and that transport ships would anchor in Copenhagen harbor on September 29 to take on Jews who were arrested the following day.

Duckwitz returned to Copenhagen, but on September 25 he flew to Stockholm, Sweden, to ask the neutral Swedish government if they would take Danish Jews in the near future. Although Duckwitz was not given a definite commitment at that time, the Swedes were alerted and made their preparations. The Swedish Prime Minister was able to promise that his government would accept the 8,000 Danish Jews if the German government approved their emigration. The Swedish plan was to send their offer in a telegram to Berlin and then discreetly notify Duckwitz of his government's decision through their embassy in Copenhagen.

By September 29, Duckwitz was certain that his government had decided to decline the Swedish offer, and intended to proceed with the roundup of the Jews. It was then that Duckwitz made a fateful decision regarding the Jews of Denmark: he turned traitor to his government. Duckwitz went to the headquarters of the Social Democratic Party at 22 Roemer Street in Copenhagen and informed the leader, Hans Hedtoft, that the disaster was but twenty-four hours away.

Hedtoft at first tried to warn C.B. Henriques, who was the head of the Jewish community in Copenhagen (hence, also of all Denmark). Henriques found the news impossible to believe, and in fact he called Hedtoft a liar. Only the day before, Henriques had been assured by the Danish Prime Minister that no action was contemplated against the Jews by the German authorities. But the Prime Minister was misled.

The Social Democrats were rebuffed by Henriques, but they resolved to warn every Jew they could locate. Word spread rapidly among the gentiles to warn the Jews. Marchus Melchior, rabbi of the Copenhagen synagogue, was less incredulous than his colleague Henriques, so he warned his congregation when they assembled for Rosh Hashana services. At first, the people received the news in stunned disbelief, but as the truth dawned on them, they heeded their rabbi's direction to go into hiding at once.

The warning went out extremely fast, especially considering that radio broadcasts were not available to them and telephones were dangerous. (Only public telephones could be used because all telephone lines were routinely monitored by the Germans and could be traced.)

All during the day of warning, thousands of Christians and Jews warned those who had not heard the news. Christians from all walks of life took time from their normal pursuits to warn and take into hiding the Jews of their communities. Many Jews were hidden with Christian friends, while many others found refuge with complete strangers.

Rabbi Melchior called a Lutheran pastor, Hans Kildeby, who lived in the town of Oerslev about sixty miles from Copenhagen. When asked to take one or two of the rabbi's five children, Kildeby insisted on taking the whole family. The rabbi cautioned Kildeby that he faced prison if they were caught, but the pastor replied "(I am) . . . ready for prison." Melchior arranged with another pastor to hide the Scriptures and sacred objects from the synagogue.

The response of the Danes was spontaneous and effective. Ambulance driver Jorgen Knudsen was typical of the nation. He was driving to work when he noticed some of his friends running through the streets. He stopped them and asked what was happening. Knudsen didn't know any Jews, so he went to a nearby telephone booth and ripped out the directory. He circled every Jewish name he could find and then proceeded to deliver the warning. In many cases, Knudsen found that the frantic Jews had no place to hide, so he loaded them into his ambulance and drove them to Bispebjerg Hospital where he knew Dr. K.H. Koester was willing to hide them. All over Denmark, Jewish patients in hospitals suddenly "recovered" and were officially discharged, only to be immediately readmitted under gentile names.

Mendel Katlev left his place of business to return home after learning of the impending raid. The distraught Katlev must have shown on his face the dread that was in his heart, because a train conductor named Carstensen inquired if he were ill. Katlev told the conductor the bad news, lamenting that he didn't know where he would go. ". . . to my house!" exclaimed Carstensen. The train conductor took the Katlev family into his home despite the fact that he didn't even know them. In fact, the two men didn't even know each other's names until Katlev got off the train.

The Rosh Hashana roundup on October 1, 1943, was a failure for the Germans. Only 202 Jews were netted the first day, and the total climbed to only 472 by November 1: the rest of Denmark's 8,000 Jews escaped into hiding. Most of the 270 who were captured after Rosh Hashana were caught in their disorganized flight to the coast. They were hoping to escape to Sweden in boats, so they risked traveling at a time when the underground railroad was not yet established.

All over Denmark, Jews went into hiding to avoid capture by the Germans. They found refuge in homes, in offices, on farms, in hospitals and in places of business. Overnight the Jewish population disappeared. The overconfident Dr. Best sent Hitler and Ribbontrop a self-congratulatory telegram proclaiming that Denmark was *Judenrein* (free of Jews)—it was a boast occasioned by his earlier treatment by Hitler, but that he was to regret making!

But what could be done with the Jews? It would prove impossible to keep all 8,000 Jews safely hidden until the Germans departed. Emigration out of Denmark to a neutral country was the only viable solution to the problem of saving the Danish Jews. Sweden was the logical choice because of its neutrality, and the fact that only two miles of sea separate the two countries at their closest points.

But Sweden was painfully aware of the German presence just across the border in Norway. The Swedish government proceeded warily on any matter that would antagonize the Germans. Even though by 1943 the government of Sweden had detailed knowledge of the Final Solution, they were still reluctant to offend the Germans. They were acutely aware that "Jewish matters" were of prime importance to the Germans, and that Hitler would not look kindly on Swedish interference in his plans. Sweden closed its borders to Norwegian Jews escaping the Nazis through the forests and mountains that link their country to Sweden: the result was disaster for the Jewish community in Norway. The possibility of using Sweden as a refuge did not look promising until after Danish physicist Neils Bohr arrived in Stockholm on October 1, 1943—the day of the planned roundup of Danish Jews.

Dr. Neils Bohr was an internationally known physicist who won the Nobel Prize for his work in quantum physics. He invented the model of the atom which most people remember from their high school science classes, namely a nucleus of protons and neutrons which is surrounded by orbiting electrons. The Allies knew that Bohr was second only to Einstein, and indeed was the greater expert in his own field of quantum mechanics. His ability and knowledge were extremely important to both the Allies and the Nazis, and it was feared that he could lead the Germans to an atomic bomb ahead of the United States. Bohr was smuggled out of Denmark to Stockholm on October 1, 1943, but he refused to continue on to Britain as planned until the Swedes made a commitment to take in Jewish refugees. Social Democrat leader Hans Hedtoft warned Bohr of the dangers facing the Jews, so he sought to make an issue of it with the Swedish government.

The Swedes were placed in a bit of a predicament by Bohr's insistent demands. They did not want to alert the Germans to Bohr's presence because of the fear of kidnaping or assassination—both would be ugly international incidents. They were also concerned lest the Germans challenge their neutrality because of their help to the British in the matter. Bohr first met with the Prime Minister, but without success. An angry Neils Bohr then demanded to meet with King Gustav—a bit of chutzpah that only a Nobel Laureate could get away with in Sweden, the home of the Nobel Prize. The king averred sympathy with the plight of the Jews, but could only agree to consider the matter further with his advisors. Allied agents in Stockholm breathed a sigh of relief the next day when King Gustav sent word that his government would offer refuge to any Danish Jew who escaped. Only then did Neils Bohr consent to leave Sweden for Great Britain. He was carried across the North Sea in the bomb bay of a British *Mosquito* bomber. Because of a failure in the oxygen system, Bohr lost consciousness at high altitude but recovered once back on the ground.

The straits between Denmark and Sweden narrow to only two miles at the closest point. That geography was both a blessing and a curse. While the short distances make quick trips possible, it also makes it easier to patrol. German boats kept close watch on the waters between free Sweden and slave Denmark. Nevertheless, more than 8,000 Jewish refugees made it across the straits.

Some of the refugees made it to Sweden by train ferry. Germany badly needed rich iron ore mined in Sweden. An ore train made a daily trip across the narrow staits on a barge ferry. The ore cars went over empty and returned later in the day full of high-grade ore. Many of those supposedly empty cars made the trip with a load of refugees. Of course, for security reasons, none of the escapees spoke of the train ferry until after the war. To do so would have alerted the Germans to close that particular escape route.

Most of the refugees escaped Denmark in small fishing boats. The escapees were taken to coastal fishing towns in small groups that were passed from one safe house to another. The fishermen secreted the refugees in their boats and under cover of darkness made the run across the strait to Sweden, where the refugees were off-loaded on a friendly beach. Very few of the fishermen acted greedily toward the refugees. The going rate for the trip was about sixty dollars, even when the passenger could afford much more. If a refugee didn't have the money, then most fishermen made the trip for free. Only a few tried to enrich themselves from the Jews, and they were for the most part ostracized into repentance.

The plight of the Jews who were captured—the hapless 472—was different. The Germans sent them to Theresienstadt Concentration Camp in Czechoslovakia. But they were more fortunate than some of their campmates. The Danish government persisted in their efforts on behalf of the Jews, despite the fact that annoying the Germans had become notoriously dangerous. The public clamor for the Danish Jews was a factor in keeping them alive throughout the war: of the 472 deported from Denmark, only about 50 died in the camp. Most of the dead were older or sick people who had not been able to flee and were even less able to survive the rigors of the camp.

Shortly after the deportation of the 472 Jews, officials of the Danish government went to their individual homes and fetched clothing and other items that might be needed in the camps. These were packaged and sent to the prisoners. Former employees of American Express in Copenhagen undertook the shipment of food and clothing packages to the prisoners throughout the rest of their imprisonment. These former clerks shrewdly mailed the packages with a return receipt that had to be signed by the recipient—thereby preventing theft of the packages by SS guards.

On April 13, 1945, a car bearing the Swedish flag drove into Theresienstadt with special news for the Danish Jews. A deal was made among Count Folke Bernadotte, Dr. Felix Kersten (see Chapter 10) and an increasingly nervous Heinrich Himmler under which the Danish Jews and about 2,000 other prisoners were sent aboard buses to Sweden to await the end of the war. The buses arrived at the camp and boarded the Danish Jews for the trip to Sweden by way of Copenhagen. Throngs of well-wishers scrambled around the buses as they wound their way through Copenhagen, greeting the prisoners with shouts of *Velkommen Til Danmark!* (Welcome to Denmark!).

The story of the Danish Jews is a heartwarming tale of human dignity that was all too uncommon in Europe during the Holocaust. But the story has an even more touching postlogue. All over Europe, Jewish survivors found their possessions gone, often looted by friends and neighbors who took advantage of the situation to enrich themselves. In Denmark, however, returning Jews often found their property still intact and often in better shape than when they left it. One businessman found that his employees had continued to operate the business during his absence and in the process had earned considerable profits. All during the war his employees deposited the proceeds from the business in a secret bank account under a false name. When the grateful owner returned, he found his funds intact and increased. The Jewish owners of houses and apartments found that others had occupied their premises during their absence, but moved out when the former occupants were about to return. In most cases, they found their homes in at least as good shape as when they left. One man returned to his apartment and found it intact. On the mantelpiece was a note and some money—the note indicated that the money was to pay for a bathroom tile that the occupant had accidentally broken.

There is no doubt that the toll of Jewish dead in the Holocaust would be much lower if more people had acted like the Danes. The Danish experience offers evidence that bold stands by the civil and religious leadership could have thwarted or at least impeded German plans for the extermination of the Jewish people.

7

Kurt Gerstein: God's Spy in the SS?

It was late August 1942 when an uneasy meeting took place in the corridor of an ancient sleeping car on the Warsaw-Berlin Express. SS First Lieutenant Kurt Gerstein was looking for a couchette to sleep on when the conductor pointed to a seat next to a Swedish diplomat, Baron von Otter.

Neither man could find a sleeping berth in that old ". . . skeleton made of iron, glass and wood"* type of general sleeping car, so they had to sit upright in a compartment all night long. Crowded wartime conditions made it impossible for normally privileged SS officers and foreign diplomats to obtain accommodations. Baron von Otter was at first wary of the uniformed SS man who so nervously tried to make small talk. He was keenly aware that the SS routinely planted informers to spy on foreigners, and were not

---

* All quotes in this chapter, unless otherwise identified, are from *Kurt Gerstein: The Ambiguity of Good* by Saul Friedlander, Alfred A. Knopf Publishers, New York, 1969. Used by permission.

above entrapping a neutral diplomat in a compromising situation. Yet something in Gerstein's manner overcame von Otter's professional wariness. To break the ice, von Otter extended his arm in Gerstein's direction and offered him a cigarette. Gerstein accepted the offer, and reciprocated by producing his own cigarette lighter and offering to light von Otter's cigarette. In one quick motion Gerstein flicked the lighter in von Otter's face and asked ". . . may I tell you a very grim story?"

"Are you talking about the Jews?" asked the still-cautious von Otter.

"Yes," replied Gerstein, "Jews who are being killed in the East." Lieutenant Gerstein then produced his SS identity card, some written instructions from an extermination camp Commandant, and an invoice for Zyklon-B, the brand of poisonous prussic acid used in the gas chambers. In answer to von Otter's request for a personal reference, Gerstein told him to contact Bishop Doctor Otto Debelius at Bruederweg 2, Lichterfelde-West, Berlin. The bishop was Lutheran Superintendent-General, a friend of resistance leader Pastor Martin Niemoeller and a leader himself in the small Protestant anti-Nazi resistance movement. "Ask Bishop Dibelius about Kurt Gerstein," the SS Lieutenant pleaded.

SS Lieutenant Kurt Gerstein was returning to SS headquarters in Berlin after a brief inspection tour of the Belzec extermination camp in Poland. The camp Commandant had informed Gerstein that he was one of only ten or so outside people who had seen the inner workings of an extermination camp. Throughout the six to eight hours of the journey, Gerstein and von Otter huddled in the hot, muggy corridor of the sleeping car to keep away from the other passengers. Von Otter repeatedly had to warn Gerstein to keep his voice down to prevent other passengers from over-hearing their conversation. Between fits of convulsive sobbing and loud protestations about the crime being perpetrated against the Jews, Gerstein gave von Otter details of the construction of the gas chambers, operating procedures, the role of SS personnel and the collection of valuables from the victims.

Baron von Otter left the train the next morning in Berlin convinced that Gerstein would not long survive because of his mental and emotional state. He was certain that Gerstein's tortured conscience would soon betray him: the SS would arrest and execute Kurt Gerstein.

The story of Kurt Gerstein is among the strangest of the Holocaust. He was both a physician and a mining engineer. Because of his dual profession, Gerstein was assigned to the SS Disinfection Service. In that position, he designed apparatus and supplied technical expertise concerning disinfection and hygiene for the *Waffen-SS* field troops.

The principal disinfection agent used at that time was prussic acid, which under the tradename Zyklon-B was also used to kill Jews in the concentration camps. Because of his technical expertise, Kurt Gerstein found himself in a position to witness the destruction of the Jews. He also had to process camp orders for supplies of Zyklon-B, and several times actually delivered the deadly gas himself.

But he was also a thoroughly committed evangelical

Christian. Lutheran Bishop Otto Dibelius called Gerstein ". . . a convinced Christian." Pastor Niemoeller, who formed the Confessional Church in opposition to Nazism, termed Gerstein "peculiar," but absolutely pure and "straight as a die." And therein lies the paradox of Kurt Gerstein, a paradox which makes it difficult to determine whether Kurt Gerstein was a Righteous Gentile, or just another guilty bureaucratic cog in the SS killing machine.

In the denazification trials after the war (1950), the Tubingen Denazification Court denounced Gerstein posthumously for his role in the Final Solution. The court took note of Gerstein's resistance activities, but condemned him on the weight of seemingly over-whelming "objective" evidence. It would take another fifteen years for Gerstein's family to convince the Baden-Wurttemberg state authorities to reverse the decree. On January 20, 1965, Kurt Kiesinger, the state premier, reversed the earlier decision against former SS Lieutenant Kurt Gerstein.

Who was Kurt Gerstein? What did he do, and why? What is the reason for the official equivocation toward him for so many years? Understanding Gerstein in large measure helps us understand other Germans who succumbed to Hitler.

Kurt Gerstein was born sixth in a family of seven children. The family was of long standing in Muenster, Lower Saxony, having their residence in that vicinity since the sixteenth century. The Gersteins were of the middle class of minor officials, and Kurt's father was a judge. The family bragged that it was of pure Germanic ("Aryan") stock.

Like most German Protestants of the era, Kurt Gerstein was brought up in an intensely authoritarian, hyperpatriotic atmosphere that was extremely nationalistic. The Gersteins were "very proper" Germans who were at the center of German Protestantism.

Kurt was from his earliest youth somewhat different from the other boys in the family. He was ". . . an impulsive and passionate idealist who had always been the black sheep of the family." Even later in World War II, Gerstein was at odds with his father over loyalty to the Nazi state. Gerstein was an adventurous, intellectually curious young man who became a committed Christian during his later years at school.

As a young man, Kurt joined the German Association of Christian Students, Evangelical Youth Movement, and the Federation of German Bible Circles. He was a youth leader, and directed Bible circles in Hagen, Aachen and Berlin-Charlottenberg. Gerstein's church associates found that he was a dynamic leader whose attraction for youth was ". . . difficult to describe."

The Protestantism that enveloped Germans in the twenties and thirties was mostly Lutheran, with some minor mixture of other sects. The German Protestant movement was intensely nationalistic and authoritarian. Most Protestants lamented the downfall of the old monarchy, and only passively supported the Weimar Republic. Their passive neglect of the republican government was said to "mask latent hostility" toward that government. The body of German Protestants would have welcomed a return to the monarchy that tumbled after World War I; when Hitler rose to power, most Protestant pastors were delighted. The Evangelical Church extended a "grateful welcome" the the National Socialist state, while Pastor Niemoeller (who later was interned in a concentration camp for anti-Nazi resistance) considered the ascension of the Nazis "a joyful day, a day that evokes hope."

But there were also other forces acting on German Protestantism. A large portion of the clergy was infected with the liberal theology that became the vogue in Germany during the 19th century. Saul Friedlander, whose book *Kurt Gerstein: The Ambiguity of Good* is one of the definitive works on Gerstein, tells us that ". . . the spiritual receptivity of the German Protestants to National Socialism was further strengthened by the structural weakness of their faith." The German Protestants were not only too weak to seriously resist the National Socialists, but actively welcomed them. When Kurt Gerstein joined the Nazi Party on May 2, 1933, he was acting entirely in accord with the normal practice of other Protestants within his own society.

It wasn't long, however, before Kurt Gerstein's faith brought him into fundamental opposition to his own church and the party. The Gestapo became interested in him almost as soon as he joined the party, and started investigating him in June 1933. On October 2, 1936, Kurt Gerstein was formally expelled from the Nazi Party for "Christian activities directed against the Nazi state."

An incident that contributed to Gerstein's expulsion from the party occurred at the Municipal Theatre in Hagen, Westphalia. An anti-Christian play titled *Wittekind* was playing. On the second anniversary of

Hitler's rise to power, January 30, 1935, a noisy demonstration occurred at the theater when Catholic youths attending the play objected to its anti-Christian content. The next day, the mayor issued a strong warning that further outbreaks would not be tolerated, but that evening the play was again interrupted by a lone demonstrator: Kurt Gerstein. When an actor spoke the lines "We want no savior who weeps and laments!" Kurt Gerstein jumped to his feet and shouted "This is unheard of! We shall not allow our faith to be publicly mocked without protest!" Uniformed party members on either side of him attacked Gerstein, causing him to lose several teeth and suffer an eye injury.

On September 27, 1936, Gerstein was imprisoned by the Gestapo for the crime of distributing anti-Nazi Christian literature to government employees. He remained in prison until the end of October. Because of his imprisonment, Gerstein was excluded from employment by the government.

Gerstein's profession at that time was mining engineering, which meant that exclusion from the state service denied him the means for making a living. Very few positions existed for mining engineers outside of the government. Gerstein found it necessary, therefore, to change professions. For a while he studied theology at Tubingen, but soon gave up that discipline for medicine. Gerstein entered medical school at the Protestant Missions Institute for Tropical Medicine in Tubingen.

During the time of his studies in Tubingen, Gerstein married a pastor's daughter named Elfriede Bensch and continued agonizing over the ethical condition into which his country was falling. He continued to print and distribute anti-Nazi religious pamphlets, for which he was once again arrested. From July 14 to August 28, 1938, Gerstein was a prisoner in the Welzheim Concentration Camp. He entertained the idea of emigrating from Germany, but gave up the idea.

Adding to Gerstein's disenchantment with the Nazi regime was Hermann Rauschning's book *Hitler Speaks* (published in the USA under the title *The Voice of Destruction*). This book was banned in Germany, but was passed secretly "from hand to hand." Rauschning had been a confidant of Hitler from 1929 to 1934, when he left Germany for England in disillusionment. He had been privy to Hitler's private life, and was a frequent guest in Hitler's home. Rauschning was among the earliest and most reliable witnesses of Nazi occultism, and reported on it in his book. To a devoted Christian like Kurt Gerstein, occultism was evidence of satanic involvement. Gerstein was introduced to the book in Holland, and carried it back to Germany with him and passed it to Pastor Niemoeller's Confessional Church resistance group.

Gerstein Joins the SS

Given Gerstein's record of anti-Nazi activity, it is something of a miracle that he was accepted at all by the *Waffen-SS*. He was, after all, expelled from the Nazi Party in 1936. But he was accepted, and on March 10, 1941, Kurt Gerstein formally joined Hitler's elite. Oddly enough, it was the two Gestapo agents who had been following his case, and who were responsible for his imprisonment, who aided him in making his application to SS authorities. Their motives for doing so seem obscure to us today, but actually provide some insight into the totalitarian mind. Although they previously had persecuted Gerstein for his Christian activity, they were apparently pleased that he had "come around," and was now a "good German"; especially since the Gersteins boasted of pure Aryan blood and Kurt's father was a judge in service to the state. One of the Gestapo men remarked to him that ". . . an idealist like you should make a fanatical member of the Party."

But the potential Nazi fanatic was really engaged in spying on the SS. Although some writers indicate that Gerstein's motives for joining the *Waffen-SS* are ambiguous, it is clear that the primary cause for his decision was the murder of his mentally ill sister-in-law, Bertha Ebeling, by the SS in 1940.

Sometime around September 1939, just as World War II was beginning with the German invasion of Poland, Adolf Hitler ordered the murder of mental patients and the mentally retarded. Some sources claim that Hitler got the idea from a letter sent in by a father requesting that the Fuehrer kill his child, supposedly "for her own good." That letter might have been the immediate stimulus in September 1939, but the executions were carried out under a hideous act passed earlier by the Nazis: the infamous "Law for the Destruction of Lives Not Worth Living."

The euthanasia program was kept extremely secret. It was of such great secrecy that administration of the program was not delegated to the general SS bureaucracy, but was instead controlled directly by the Fuehrer's staff in the *Reichschancellory*. According to Friedlander, the euthanasia program was ". . . camouflaged with meticulous care."

Police Inspector Christian Wirth, Superintendent of the Criminal Investigation Division (KRIPO) of the Stuttgart Police, was selected to carry out the program. By the end of 1939, Inspector Wirth had the first killing center in operation at Brandenberg. Five other murder centers were placed in operation during 1940, including the facilities at Grafeneck and Hadamar.

The euthanasia program was a grisly predecessor to the Holocaust. The first patients killed at Brandenberg were killed by shots in the head from small-caliber military pistols. But shooting proved too slow, and, oddly enough, was distasteful to the murderers.

Wirth soon turned his attention to devising a more efficient means of execution. He acquired the early technical expertise that was to prove so useful a year later when the killing of Jews began: gas chambers were installed.

Two different means of killing were used in the gas-chamber phase of the euthanasia program; both used carbon monoxide gas as the killing agent. In one type of facility, the gas was stored in tanks that were connected to the gas chambers through a system of pipes. In the other type of facility, the exhaust from a diesel engine was channeled into the chamber. The engine was mounted on a fixed stand outside the killing shed, and was started as soon as the doors were sealed on the hapless victims inside.

In both types of facility, the gas chamber was camouflaged as either a shower or a disinfection station. But unlike those benign facilities, the euthanasia chambers were hermetically sealed to contain the deadly gas.

The victims were patients of mental hospitals and homes for the mentally retarded. Some sources claim that the program also killed certain physically handicapped persons. The victims were drugged with soporifics, morphine or scopolomine before being taken to the death chamber. The drowsy victims were herded two to twenty at a time into the gas chamber and the doors were sealed behind them. Thirty minutes later, all were dead.

During the twenty months that the program operated, a total of 70,273 mental patients and retarded persons were executed in the six killing centers. Gerstein's sister-in-law was one of those victims, and her death forced him into his decision to join the *Waffen-SS*. He recalled that several times SS Security Department (SS-SD) undercover agents had penetrated his own Confessional Church unit to inform on the members, so he felt "if they can do it, so can I!" Although his pastor was aghast at the idea, and advised him not to join, Kurt Gerstein's mind was made up.

Gerstein's suspicions regarding his sister-in-law's death were fueled by rumors circulating in Germany at the time, and by the Lutheran Bishop of Stuttgart, who told Gerstein that Bertha Ebeling had been murdered by the SS. Although the program was classified as a Highest Reichs Secret, it was general knowledge. So much was known of the program that children playing in Hadamar would shout "here comes another load to be gassed" when the buses bringing victims to the sanitarium rolled through town. It was a combination of the high death rate at sanitariums, indiscretions by officials involved in the programs, and the sickly sweet odor of the crematoria that gave the program away. The bodies were cremated in order to prevent independent medical analysis from determining the true cause of death. The families were told that the patient died of natural causes, and the Nazis did not want any private physician contradicting the official statement: the families were usually told that heart failure, pneumonia or influenza caused the patient's death. If a small killing program such as the euthanasia effort could not be kept secret, then it is easier to understand how widespread—contrary to popular opinion and the claims of many Germans today—was knowledge of the Holocaust. Dr. Walter Laqueur's book *The Terrible Secret* and Dr. Martin Gilbert's *Auschwitz and the Allies* lay to rest rather conclusively the question of who, and how many, knew what was happening to the Jews. It is a shame for Christians that there are so few Righteous Gentiles!

Gerstein began his SS career by taking ten weeks (March 10-June 2) of basic military training with a class of forty other doctors at the SS training centers in Hamburt-Langehoorn, Oranienburg and Arnheim. While most of the doctors were destined for *Waffen-SS* field hospitals, Gerstein's dual professions of engineering and medicine caused him to be selected for a medical-technical post in the *Waffen-SS Amtsgruppe D,* Hygeine. He was quickly put to work devising apparatus for mass disinfection and for water filtration. These apparatus were needed in the concentration camps and in the field by *Waffen-SS* combat units. This task was complicated, and several predecessors failed to design workable units. But Gerstein's industrial experience gave him a unique edge over other doctors, and he rapidly succeeded. His quick success earned him commendations and a promotion.

The principal disinfectant used in those days was a pest-control agent called prussic acid. A slightly different form of prussic acid was used to kill Jews in the death camps, where it was known under the Degesch Organization trade name Zyklon-B.

The SS career of Kurt Gerstein almost came to an early end in November 1941, before his first anniversary in the service. He attended the funeral of his brother Alfred in Hamm. During his visit he was seen in uniform by one of the judges of the National Socialist Party Court which had expelled him in 1936. The judge notified the *Waffen-SS* High Command that an "undesirable" was in its ranks and stated the Party's demand that Gerstein be expelled from the service.

But Gerstein's technical expertise was of immense value to the SS, and his superiors were steadfast in their support of him. He had, after all, succeeded where others failed, so his superiors were interested in retaining him for the good of the SS. They maintained that Gerstein was a "good German," who was "thoroughly rehabilitated." Following this incident, Gerstein knew that he could not stumble, even slightly, so he put on the appearance of being a "German's German," and the very essence of the nordic beast that

Himmler fantasized to be the core of the SS. Some former SS men testified after the war that Gerstein was hard, and coming from Berlin headquarters, terrified them when he visited their facilities.

Shortly after he weathered the challenge to his right to remain in the SS, Kurt Gerstein was appointed head of the *Waffen-SS* Technical Disinfection Service—the office that handled toxic gases. He took his new—and ultimately fateful—job in January 1942.

The "Final Solution"

In June 1941, Hitler's "Final Solution to the Jewish Problem" began with the slaughter of Jews were who trapped in the former Soviet territories captured by the German army. Four SS Special Action Units (*SS-Einsatzgruppen*), numbering 500 to 900 men each, followed the *Wehrmacht* into Russia, the Ukraine and the Baltic countries occupied by the Soviets. SS Special Action troops rounded up the Jews and executed them with machine-gun fire. By January 1942, when Gerstein was made head of the disinfection department of the SS, more than 600,000 Jews were dead.

But killing is not part of the normative values of Europeans, even graduates of SS hate schools. Morale in the Special Action Units plummeted to dangerously low levels as the killing progressed. The top SS commander, *Reichsfuehrer-SS* Heinrich Himmler, made a tour of the murder units in an effort to bolster sagging morale. The SS troopers found the shooting of Jews repulsive, but continued the murders out of a sense of duty—even if a hateful duty that was a "necessary cleansing action."

Himmler witnessed a mass execution while on his tour. After the machine-gunners finished their deadly work, Himmler accompanied the squad commander to the rim of the open-pit mass grave to watch while survivors were finished off with pistol and submachine-gun fire. But when the officer fired his pistol into the head of a survivor, some blood and brain tissue splattered Himmler's uniform. The squeamish *Reichs-fuehrer-SS* turned nauseous and fainted into the arms of his adjutant, SS Captain Karl Wolff. The captain turned to the squad commander and remarked: "It is good that the *Reischsfuehrer* has seen this hated bloody business, so he knows what he expects our men to do." Shortly after his Russian trip, Himmler ordered that another means of killing be found.

Subsequent to the Himmler order, Gerstein received a visit from a man wearing civilian clothes who was introduced as SS Major Rolf Guenther, an officer in the SS Reichs Central Security Department, or RSHA. It was from RSHA desk IV.b.4 that SS Lieutenant Colonel Adolf Eichmann carried out the orders relating to the Final Solution, and Guenther was Eichmann's deputy. Guenther ordered Gerstein to acquire 100 kilograms (220 pounds) of Zyklon-B (prussic acid) for a top-secret mission. Gerstein was told to personally take the prussic acid to a place in Czechoslovakia known only to the driver of the truck that would be placed at his disposal. Gerstein later viewed this mission as a God-sent opportunity to witness things that had previously been seen only by guilty participants.

Within time, Gerstein became the SS bureaucrat to deal with the Degesch Organization in Hamburg (manufacturer of Zyklon-B). This connection was primarily what caused the Denazification Courts to posthumously denounce him after the war. While he procured much of the gas used to murder the Jews, he was also ". . . in a position to prevent a great deal." Gerstein routinely diverted or destroyed large quantities of Zyklon-B, enough to kill as many as 11,000,000 people!

Trip to Poland

On August 15, 1942, Adolf Hitler and Heinrich Himmler toured the Belzec Extermination Camp, which was located on the Lublin-Lwow railroad line in Poland. Belzec was opened the previous March by Police Inspector Wirth, the same man who gained his deadly expertise in the 1939-41 Euthanasia Program. The Belzec gas chambers used the same sort of carbon monoxide mechanism as the gas chambers in the Euthanasia Program.

Hitler ordered that ". . . things be speeded up" at Belzec, so Wirth had to find a new and more potent killing agent . . . such as prussic acid. It was only a matter of hours before Gerstein received his order to acquire 220 pounds of the deadly gas and deliver it to a location "known only to the driver of the truck."

Gerstein's trip took him from Berlin to the Degesch plant in Kolin, Czechoslovakia (where the gas was made), and then to Belzec. Accompanying Gerstein on the trip was Professor Pfannenstiel (Professor of Hygiene at the University of Marburg-Lahn). The pair took possession of the prussic acid in Kolin, and then on August 17, 1942, reported to SS Brigadier General Odilo Globocnik in Lublin.

General Globocnik warned Gerstein and Pfannenstiel that the camp's work was one of the "Reich's Most Secret matters," perhaps ". . . the *most* secret. The two visitors were warned that people who talked about the camps would be shot. "Yesterday," warned Globocnik, "two more who couldn't keep their mouths shut were shot."

Gerstein and Pfannenstiel were told that the SS had three camps in operation, one under construction and several more to be converted to extermination camps in the near future. Belzec could kill 15,000 people a day, Treblinka (75 miles north-northeast of Warsaw) could kill 25,000 people a day, and Sobibor could kill 20,000 a day; altogether, these three early camps had the capacity to murder 60,000 Jews per day—yet Hitler wanted ". . . things speeded up"!

The Maidanek camp was almost ready to start killing that August, while Auschwitz (eventually the primary death camp) was being converted from a work camp to an extermination camp. More than 2,000,000 people eventually died in Auschwitz alone.

The SS had two assignments for Gerstein. First, he was to construct the apparatus needed to disinfect the mountains of garments and other textiles that were stolen from the murdered victims. Second, Gerstein was to improve the gas chambers to allow use of Zyklon-B instead of carbon monoxide (which suffered the dual disadvantage of taking too long to kill and being generated by burning diesel fuel needed by Germany's mechanized armies).

After their interview with General Globocnik, Gerstein and Pfannenstiel were taken to the Belzec Extermination Camp. The train station at Belzec was on the south side of the tracks and bore a simple sign: *Waffen-SS,* Belzec Office. On the day that Gerstein arrived, there were no executions, but a sickly sweet odor from the crematoria permeated the district and told the tale of the day before. The next morning, a forty-five car train loaded with 6,000 Jews arrived from Lemberg; almost 1,500 were already dead from the rigors of the journey.

A force of 200 armed Ukrainian *Waffen-SS* Foreign Auxiliaries tore open the cattle-car doors, shouting *"Juden Raus!"* (Jews out!). They drove the terrified victims out of the cars with long, rawhide whips; the victims stumbled and jostled their way out of the cramped train cars and headed for a large hut marked "Cloak Room" on the north side of the tracks. All the while, a loudspeaker barked orders to deposit all belongings in wicker baskets marked "Valuables." Women and girls were herded into a room marked "Hairdresser" where in a quick stroke or two their hair was shorn off. The hair was used to stuff mattresses, and to make felt slippers for U-boat crews. (U-boat crews needed to walk quietly in order to avoid detection by U.S. Navy underwater hydrophones.)

After the victims were stripped naked and their hair shorn, they were forced out of the cloak room building into a 150-yard-long alley that was lined with barbed wire. All along the alley were signs reading "To Baths and Inhalation Rooms."

The four sixteen-by-sixteen-foot gas chambers were disguised as a bathhouse; to the left and right of the pathway were potted geraniums, and on the roof was the most cynical deception of all: a large copper Star of David.

The march from the cloak room to the gas chambers took only a few minutes. All along the route there were Ukrainian Auxiliaries armed with rifles and sub-machine guns; a burly SS Sergeant kept bellowing the lie "Nothing terrible is going to happen to you!" Most of the victims knew what was going to happen, but some still held out hope that the SS man was telling them the truth. "Breathe deeply!" hollered the SS man, "Inhalation is a good means of preventing infection." One woman, about forty years of age, ran up to the group of SS officers witnessing the executions and called down on them curses for the blood being shed there; others wailed the Jewish lament "who will give us water to wash the dead?"

Inspector Wirth was proud to show off his technique to General Globocnik and his visiting dignitaries from Berlin (Gerstein, Pfannenstiel and Rolf Guenther). More than 3,000 people, almost 800 victims in each of the four 1500-cubic-foot gas chambers, were crushed into the "bathhouse": men, women, children and infants alike without mercy. But Wirth's pride soon turned to terror as he realized that the mass execution was turning into a disaster for him. SS Sergeant Heckenholt and his Ukrainian assistant were unable to start the diesel engine that generated the carbon monoxide. Gerstein contemptuously took out a stop-watch and began timing the proceedings, while a frantic Wirth began whipping the Ukrainian and cursing Heckenholt. Time dragged on for forty, fifty, and then seventy minutes and the recalcitrant engine still would not start. Throughout the entire ghoulish period, Gerstein could hear the wails of the terror-stricken victims locked in the chambers. Finally, after two hours, forty-nine minutes, Heckenholt managed to start the engine and carbon monoxide started pouring into the gas chambers. Thirty-two minutes later, all of the victims were dead of asphixiation.

Other Jewish prisoners removed the bodies from the chambers and took them to the crematoria for burning; but not before the corpses were searched in the most intimate places for gold, currency and jewels. A Jewish dentist salvaged gold teeth, while a jeweler inventoried and evaluated other booty. All through the proceedings an old Jewish man lent a surrealistic air to the murders by playing his violin. Inspector Wirth told Gerstein that the old man was allowed to live temporarily because in World War I he won the *Knights Cross of the Iron Cross* (a medal roughly equivalent to the Medal of Honor).

Gerstein later recounted his feelings at what he had witnessed at Belzec:

> I prayed with them. I pressed myself into a corner and cried out to my God and theirs. How glad I should have been to go into the gas chambers with them! How gladly I should have died the same death as theirs! Then an SS officer in uniform would have been found in the gas chambers. People

would have believed it was an accident and the story would have been buried and forgotten. But I could not do this yet. I felt I must not succumb to the temptation to die with these people. I now knew a great deal about these murders. Wirth had told me, "There are not ten people alive who have seen, or will see, as much as you." When the whole thing was over, all the foreign auxiliaries would be executed. I was one of the handful of people who had seen every corner of the establishment, and certainly the only one to have visited it as an enemy of this gang of murderers.

Following the tour of Belzec, Wirth took Gerstein to Treblinka, which was then the largest death camp. It was located about seventy-five miles north-northeast of Warsaw, and was set up specifically to exterminate the large Jewish population of the Warsaw Ghetto. The Treblinka Death Camp used the same kind of equipment as Belzec, but was much larger: 25,000 people per day could be gassed in its thirty-two gas chambers. Gerstein saw a "mountain of clothing and underwear, 115 to 130 feet high," all stolen from the victims. That evening, at a banquet held in honor of the guests from Berlin, Dr. Pfannenstiel, Professor of Hygiene at the University of Marburg-Lahn, made a speech: "The work you are doing is great work and a duty so useful and so necessary."

When his tour was completed, he had seen the inner workings of the two main death camps (he did not visit

Sobibor) that were then in operation. On his return to Berlin a few nights later, the tormented Gerstein had his historic encounter with the Swedish diplomat, Baron von Otter.

Later, when a Christian friend and pastor asked Gerstein how he could stand by and watch such horrible events, Gerstein replied: "Events are taking their inexorable and logical course. I am glad to have seen these atrocities with my own eyes, so that one day I may be able to testify about them."

Gerstein attempted to take the story of the Holocaust to the Allies and the neutrals. Shortly after the von Otter encounter, Gerstein tried without success to see the Papal Nuncio (ambassador) in Berlin. About a year later, von Otter encountered Gerstein on the street and told him that his information had been passed to the Swedish government, but there was little that could be done.

Thereafter, Kurt Gerstein lived a tormented existence; while trying to camouflage himself as an ideal SS Technical-Medical Officer, he also attempted to sabotage the extermination program by "losing" and diverting tons of Zyklon-B. On one occasion, he buried fifteen tons of the deadly gas crystals in Czechoslovakia on grounds that the crystals were dangerously decomposed.

On another occasion in late 1944, he diverted a huge quantity of Zyklon-B ordered for some top-secret purpose by Rolf Guenther. Only a short time before, *Reichsminister* for Propaganda and Enlightenment Dr. Josef Goebbels had stated that "[we will slam] the doors behind us in Nazism goes under." Gerstein suspected that this statement meant that the prussic acid ordered by Guenther would be used to kill all remaining concentration camp prisoners, prisoners of war and large numbers of German civilians (such an event was possible, for Adolf Hitler had ordered a scorched-earth policy after the failures of the Ardennes Offensive—"The Battle of the Bulge"—in December 1944). Gerstein disposed of many metric tons of gas, enough to kill more than 8,000,000 people, and it was never delivered to Guenther.

Shortly thereafter, Berlin came under final attack by the Russians. In January 1945, Adolf Hitler and his entourage of "Mountain People" descended 55 feet into the *Fuehrerbunker* that was buried beneath the *Reichschancellory* garden for the 105-day countdown to the end of his life. On April 30, 1945, only a few hours after marrying Eva Braun, Adolf Hitler and his bride consummated their marriage with potassium cyanide and pistol shots to the head. Hitler, who was born in 1889 on the eve of Easter Sunday, committed suicide on Walpurgis Night—satanism's highest holiday.

The End for Kurt Gerstein

Germany surrendered unconditionally on May 8, 1945, only a week after Hitler's death. All over Europe that week, hundreds of thousands of emaciated concentration camp inmates were rescued and given food and medical treatment by the Allies. Many thousands died, even after rescue, too exhausted by Hitler's hatred to continue any longer.

Thousands of former SS personnel tried to disappear into the grey-green mass of the defeated German army. Many SS criminals donned the uniforms of low-ranking *Wehrmacht* troopers and mingled with the surrendering troops. Some escaped altogether and wound up in the Middle East or South America. Some, like arch-criminal Heinrich Himmler, falsely believed that only the higher ranks of the SS were wanted by the Allies, so they donned lower-ranking SS uniforms and were caught. Himmler and others were not aware that the Allies were arresting anyone in any SS uniform, so he blithely walked into a trap at a British roadblock while wearing the uniform of an SS Security Service (SS-SD) corporal. He soon collapsed under interrogation and admitted his identity, but shortly thereafter committed suicide with a cyanide ampule hidden on his body. It is, perhaps, ironically fitting that one of the officers engaged in Himmler's capture was a Palestinian Jew serving in the British Army: Chaim Herzog, who later became a general in the Israeli Defense Forces, a statesman, and a diplomat for the State of Israel.

While other SS men were fleeing the Allies, Gerstein surrendered voluntarily in the hopes that he would be able to testify about what he had seen. In May, 1945, Gerstein surrendered to French forces in Germany, and shortly thereafter was taken to the Cherche-Midi Military Prison in Paris—a damp, vermin-infested jail that the French reserved for their former tormentors.

The French interrogated Gerstein from May until July 1945, and it is on the basis of this testimony that we know about his activities. Gerstein wrote to his wife that he was eager to testify against the criminals who operated the death camps, and that he would rejoin her when it was all over.

But it was all over sooner than Kurt Gerstein's letters indicated: late in the day of July 25, 1945, SS Lieutenant Kurt Gerstein was found hanged in his cell. Although the French military authorities ruled his death a suicide, there are too many unexplained riddles to accept that conclusion.

First, Gerstein's attitude in his letters to his wife was positive and full of hope for the future: he was finally going to bring action against the murderers who destroyed the Jews.

Second, French authorities claimed that they had letters in their possession in which Gerstein expressed suicidal intent. But these letters have never been produced, and the French claim that they were lost.

Third, Gerstein was buried a week later (August 3, 1945) in an obscure Paris cemetery under a false name (Gastein) that may have been an error, or possibly intentional.

Finally, no one notified the Gerstein family of Gerstein's death. For three years the family was uncertain as to his fate, despite their continued efforts at finding his whereabouts. It was not until 1948 that the French admitted that Kurt Gerstein died while in their custody.

While it is possible that the tormented mind of Kurt Gerstein led him to commit suicide, that is unlikely. What seems more likely is that he was murdered in prison. That prison was used mostly to house captured SS men, and most of them were still unrepentant Nazis (as many are Nazis even today!). When word got around the prison that Gerstein was testifying against them, it is probable that some of those unrepentant thugs killed him to keep him from testifying against them—many were guilty of crimes during the war.

As for the French, their strange behavior might be explained as embarrassment over not realizing the value of Gerstein's testimony in time and their failure to protect so valuable a catch.

The Lesson of Kurt Gerstein

Kurt Gerstein presents an enigma to the student of the Holocaust. Was he truly a committed Christian "spying on the SS," as he and others claimed? Or was Kurt Gerstein just another Nazi thug who invented a clever story to cover his own culpability? Or, possibly, was Kurt Gerstein a committed Christian who backslid into the sin of Nazism after being caught up in the nationalistic and racist euphoria of the Hitler movement?

Saul Friedlander's subtitle for his biography of Kurt Gerstein is an apt selection: . . . *The Ambiguity of Good*. Friedlander's analysis of Gerstein is probably more accurate than any other:

> If resistance within the body of a totalitarian system is ambiguous by its very nature, one criterion nonetheless remains essential for defining it: that of the danger incurred. There were many Germans who put forward the argument that they had resisted inside the system to explain away their participation in Nazi activities. Yet

how many of them demonstrated their will to resist by committing acts which, had they been discovered, would have cost the perpetrators their lives? Kurt Gerstein was one of these people . . .

and, to continue:

So much of Gerstein's tragedy lay in the loneliness of his action. The silence and passivity of the Germans, the absence of any notable reaction among the Allies and the neutrals, indeed, in the Christian West as a whole, in the face of the extermination of the Jews, invests the role of Gerstein with its true significance: his appeals having brought no response and his dedication having proved a solitary commitment, his sacrifice appeared "useless" and became "guilt."

In other words, while the Denazification Courts in 1950 recognized Gerstein's resistance to the Nazi system, they condemned him solely for the *uselessness* of his activities. While any righteous man would cry out at the injustice of such a condemnation, it was to be fifteen years before Gerstein's wife managed to have him exonerated. Perhaps there were too many Germans who still ached over having done nothing . . . and to them Kurt Gerstein had to remain anathema.

It is difficult to finally judge Gerstein. Do you give medals to the man who supplied Zyklon-B to Auschwitz? Perhaps, but unless more information becomes available Gerstein will have to remain a nebulous sort of righteous gentile.

Only God can judge Kurt Gerstein.

8
Felix Kersten:
The Man With the Miraculous Hands

One of the most curious tales to come out of the Holocaust is the role of Dr. Felix Kersten, a Finnish citizen who lived most of the war in Berlin, and who served as Heinrich Himmler's personal physician and confidant from 1940 to 1945. It is not known if Kersten was a Christian in the sense the term is used in this book. His story is so unique, however, that it must be told in any such as this one—otherwise, the author is guilty of the most despicable lapse of scholarship. Very little was known of Kersten in the West (even though the Swedish and Finnish governments knew of his activities) until very late in the war. Sir Hugh Trevor-Roper, one of the foremost historians of World War II, was a British intelligence officer during the war. In his introduction to Kersten's memoirs he tells us that the name "Kersten" kept coming up in interviews with captured SS officers, yet no one in British Intelligence knew anything at all about the man.

The story of Felix Kersten is astounding, for he alone was able to save the lives of hundreds of thousands of concentration camp victims, including many Jews. When, for example, a train with 2,700 hapless Jewish deportees ended up in Switzerland instead of Auschwitz (much to the joyous surprise of the victims who were, by then, fully aware of the purpose of the death camps!) it was because Heinrich Himmler was grudgingly keeping a promise made to Kersten. Imagine the absolute joy of those Jews when the train doors opened and they saw the uniforms of the Swiss Red Cross instead of the lifeless grey uniforms of the SS Death's Head Formation!

According to the account of Joseph Kessel, Kersten was solely responsible for preventing the deportation to Poland of the entire population of the Netherlands! Hitler and Himmler wanted the Dutch deported because of their resistance to the Nazis, and it was Kersten who talked *Reichsfuehrer-SS* Himmler into delaying the punishment of the Dutch people until after Germany won the war . . . which, of course, never happened.

Felix Kersten was born of Baltic German parents in 1898. When World War I broke out, he was living in the German principality of Schleswig-Holstein studying agriculture. Although considered a subject of Kaiser Wilhelm by the German government, Kersten managed to evade service in the German army by enlisting in the Finnish army. When the Finns sent a force to fight the Russians in Estonia, Kersten was with them as an officer.

After World War I ended, Kersten recovered from wounds in a Helsinki, Finland, military hospital. There he became friends with a surgeon named Major Ekman.

Kersten confessed to Ekman his own desire to become a surgeon. But Ekman could not give Kersten much hope. He told Kersten that medical training was both long and expensive, and therefore beyond the means of a man who had to support himself with work right away. Dr. Ekman looked at Kersten's powerfully built hands and recommended that he take up "scientific massage" instead of medicine.

Dr. Ekman introduced Kersten to Dr. Kollander, a Doctor of Scientific Massage who treated patients at the military hospital. Massage is an old and honored art in Finland, and is well regarded. Medical doctors in the USA regard chiropractic, our closest but not exact analogy to Kersten's discipline, as pure quackery, even though many of their Finnish colleagues hold manual healers in high esteem. Kersten studied under Dr. Kollander and others, and received his doctoral degree in manual therapy in 1921.

On the advice of his teachers, Dr. Felix Kersten moved to Berlin to further his training. There Kersten met a Chinese masseur named Dr. Ko who claimed to have studied manual healing under Buddhist monks in Tibet. From this strange little Oriental man Kersten claimed to have learned far more about diagnosis and therapy than he learned from his Finnish mentors. This Tibetan connection no doubt intrigued the occultist Heinrich Himmler, who had already imported several Tibetan monks to assist the SS Occult Bureau.

(Tibetans had emigrated to Berlin long before the rise of Hitler. They rode the wave of occultism that swept Europe in the nineteenth century, and were among the first "missionaries" of Buddhism to the West.)

By 1940, Dr. Kersten became wealthy from his practice. He kept offices in The Hague, Netherlands (where he treated members of the Dutch royal family), and in Berlin. He lived for several months at a time in his Dutch home, and then switched residence to his German estate *Harzwalde* for the next few months.

Among Kersten's Berlin clientele was a rich industrialist who gravely needed a favor from *Reichsfuehrer-SS* Heinrich Himmler. Kersten was in the industrialist's debt, not financially but morally, because the industrialist had paid him such an exorbitant voluntary fee that he was able to buy the luxurious *Harzwalde*. So when the industrialist volunteered Kersten's services to the ailing Himmler, Kersten could hardly dissent.

Heinrich Himmler was one of the top men in the Hitler regime. Indeed, he is considered the second most powerful Nazi in all of Europe. Although his official position (*Reichsfuehrer-SS*) ranks third or fourth on the official organization table, his power as head of the SS made him de facto number two. Himmler was the commander of the SS, so he controlled a vast army and police organization. The Gestapo was an agency of the SS, as was the Security Service (SS-SD); all uniformed criminal and political police reported to Heinrich Himmler. The *Waffen-SS* was a million-man army of infantry, armored units and artillery that fought alongside the regular army in field combat. The SS also operated the concentration camp system, and bore primary responsibility for the extermination of the Jews. SS Special Action Groups slaughtered Jews in Russia by machine gun, while the SS Death's Head

Formation manned the extermination camps. The extermination of the Jews was directed first by SS Lieutenant General Reinhard Heydrich, then Ernst Kaltenbrunner (following Heydrich's assassination). Heinrich Himmler was an occultist, and had direct control over all activities of the SS—millions of people lived or died at his whim.

Reichsfuehrer-SS Himmler suffered from extremely painful, sporadic, intense stomach cramps. When his seizures came, Himmler would be in debilitating pain for days at a time—not a safe condition in the byzantine world of high Nazi officialdom! None of the medical doctors consulted by Himmler were able to offer him even the slightest relief, nor could they diagnose the source of the pain.

Consider the situation: an intense abdominal pain which doctors could neither diagnose nor treat successfully. Yet Dr. Felix Kersten, who was not a medical doctor at all but a masseur, was capable of relieving the pain almost immediately, and his treatments remained effective for some time. It was through his ability to relieve Himmler's intense suffering by a few kneads of the stomach muscles that the fat, pudgy Finnish masseur was able to influence Himmler to let thousands live. Himmler once complained only half in jest that "Kersten wrenches 1,000 lives from me with every movement of his miraculous hands."

If Himmler's disease were of ordinary organic origin, then any medical doctor could have treated him, and there would have been no way to influence the SS chief. If any ordinary doctor could work the wonder for Himmler, then none would have gotten away with making the requests and demands that Kersten made. Any doctor who tried could be shot on the spot and another practitioner summoned immediately. But Felix Kersten routinely, without failure, relieved Himmler's pain. Where everyone else failed, Kersten succeeded. Surely God used this man's hands to help save the remnant.

The first person saved by Felix Kersten's intervention was one of his own friends from The Hague. The Gestapo had arrested the man and sentenced him to death. Later, Kersten saved six Swedish businessmen who had been sentenced to death for espionage activities against the Germans in Poland. Himmler freed one of the men and commuted the sentences of the others to life imprisonment. In a later incident, the SS was planning to deport the entire Dutch population to Poland as punishment for their resistance activities. The Dutch were viewed as particularly vile by the Nazis because they were a "Germanic people," yet they resisted the Nazis. The SS planned to complete the deportation by April 20, 1941, as a birthday present to Adolf Hitler. Prior to the beginning of the mass deportations, however, Himmler had multiple bouts of painful stomach cramps and repeatedly had to call on Dr. Kersten for relief. There were many important SS projects in the works during the spring of 1941, and Kersten convinced Himmler that these other activities took priority over the Dutch project. He told Himmler that his health would not survive all of the tension, and convinced him that the deportations were less important than the war effort, and could wait until after final German victory. Kersten used the occasion of Himmler's most severe attack to extract a promise to stay the execution of the Dutch people. By the end of the war, Kersten managed to convince Himmler to release or commute the sentences of many thousands of victims.

Kersten made powerful enemies within the Nazi hierarchy, among them men like Reinhard Heydrich and Ernst Kaltenbrunner, whose plans he constantly thwarted. But the protection afforded him by his special relationship with Himmler was simply too powerful for his enemies to overcome. Kersten was warned of a planned ambush on the road that ran from his country estate into Berlin. Kaltenbrunner's men were planning to ambush the doctor and machine-gun him to death. They would then tell Himmler that it was a tragic mistake caused by Kersten's driver's failure to stop at an SS roadblock. It looked safe and foolproof. But Kersten had been warned of the trap by a friend in SS headquarters, and took a different route that morning. Later, after Kersten informed Himmler of the attack plan, the enraged Himmler invited both Kersten and Kaltenbrunner to dine with him in a private railroad car which was parked on a rail siding near Hitler's headquarters in East Prussia. Himmler let Kaltenbrunner know in no uncertain terms that Kersten was important to him and that Kaltenbrunner was to keep him from all harm. Himmler informed Kaltenbrunner that he would not survive Kersten by one hour if *anything at all* happened to him . . . no matter what the source.

The entire SS was amazed at this fat man who exercised so much control over their otherwise uncontrollable boss, Heinrich Himmler. Startled guards were often perplexed at how easily Kersten could gain entrance to the *Reichsfuehrer's* office when men like SS Lieutenant General Reinhard Heydrich needed an appointment, sometimes several days in advance. One time, when Kersten was in The Hague for a few weeks to sell his Dutch property, Himmler required him to check in every day with the local Gestapo office. For several days, Kersten was received quite rudely by the local Gestapo official. Finally, when Kersten tired of the coarse treatment, he demanded that the SS officer place a call in his name to SS headquarters in Berlin and ask for *Reichsfuehrer-SS* Himmler. The sarcastic SS official complied with the demand, fully expecting the call to fail. In a few moments, the SS headquarters operator called back and informed him that the *Reichsfuehrer* was on the line for his friend, Dr. Kersten! The much chastened SS officer handed the telephone receiver to the beaming Kersten, and never again bothered him.

Kersten's control over Himmler was so great that he was able to use Himmler's personal post office box in Berlin to receive mail from the Dutch resistance! He told Himmler that the letters were from lovers in Holland, and that he did not want his wife or secretary to see them. Himmler childishly believed himself part of "our little secret," and granted Kersten permission to use his postal box. Himmler's postal box was the only one in all of Germany, except Hitler's, that was free of censorship and the prying eyes of the Gestapo. With the connivance of Himmler's Executive Secretary, Rudolf Brandt, Kersten was able to keep in close touch with the Dutch resistance movement! I suspect that a scriptwriter would reject such a scenario as too improbable, yet it happened!

Kersten also had the use of Himmler's private military telephone trunk line, and used it on several occasions to make calls from Sweden. Kersten went to Sweden several times during World War II in order to confer with the Swedish government. Himmler's number was the only telephone line in all of Nazi-occupied Europe that could be used without fear of monitoring.

After mid-1943 it became increasingly apparent that Germany would lose the war. There was a stunning series of defeats for German forces, a resurgence of the Red Army which poured across Eastern Europe in hoards, and America had been in the war for more than a year. Himmler became nervous over his future, and began to plot with Kersten to ensure his own security. In late 1944, Kersten convinced Himmler to halt the extermination program. It was not a totally successful order because of the subversive actions of fanatical Jew-killer Adolf Eichmann, but it saved lives. Kersten carried overtures from Himmler to the Allies by way of Swedish Red Cross official Count Folke Bernadotte (who later became the only neutral observer killed in the new State of Israel's war of independence). Himmler hoped in vain for a deal that would leave him at least alive after the war, perhaps even in power.

Kersten arranged one of the most bizarre meetings of World War II between Heinrich Himmler, Folke Bernadotte, and Norbert Masur, a representative of the World Jewish Congress. Masur was a Swedish Jew, yet was convinced to come to Berlin in April, 1945, by Dr. Kersten in hopes of relieving the situation of the Jews in the concentration camps. A nervous Masur arrived by airliner at Berlin's Tempelhof Airport on April 19 and was taken to Kersten's estate by Himmler aide Walter Schellenberg. When Heinrich Himmler came to the meeting the next day (Adolf Hitler's birthday), his opening remark was incredible: "It's time you Jews and we National Socialists buried the hatchet" (already six million Jews were dead!).

After the war, Kersten was investigated by the Nuremberg Tribunal and by the governments of both Sweden and The Netherlands. In all three cases, the verdict was the same: Kersten saved many thousands of lives at the extreme risk of his own life. Yet Dr. Felix Kersten failed to boast of his own exploits until the mid-1950s—he kept silent while others claimed his achievements as their own. Some of those people were Germans who wanted to reduce their own culpability for war crimes, while others were Swedes of high rank who wanted to make themselves look better to the public. Eventually, however, both the Dutch and the Swedish governments recognized Dr. Felix Kersten's accomplishments and made his story public. Kersten's memoirs were published in the mid-1950s.

9

The Henry Family
and Mademoiselle Chaumat

Late one cold October night in 1942, during the Nazi occupation of Ghent, Belgium, Abram Lipski found himself sneaking through the streets to avoid German patrols. More frightened of traveling by day than of breaking the Jewish curfew imposed by the Germans, Lipski was moving this three-year-old son Raphael to a new hiding place. The gentile couple who had taken the child into their home only a short time before had become scared, and demanded that he leave. Too embarrassed over their change of heart to face an old friend, the couple sent the toddler with another friend to the 10 P.M. meeting at the tramway platform. With the child wrapped tightly against the chilly night air, Lipski found himself wondering "what kind of people would make a man run through the streets like this with his child so that the child would not be murdered?"

Anti-Semitism was not new to Abram Lipski. He was born in 1911 in Lodz, Poland, which was one of the most bigoted regions of central Europe. Lodz was a grimy, industrial city of about 400,000 gentiles and

200,000 Jews. The Lipski family was poor, but lovingly tightknit in the manner common among Jewish communities. The anti-Semitism that they endured was the most virulent form, and it often spilled over into violence. Polish anti-Semitism of that era would be surpassed only by that of the Nazis.

Gentiles in Lodz delighted in tormenting Jews. Slogans such as "Kill the Jews" and "Christ Killer" were routinely hurled at passing Jews or scrawled on walls where Jews were bound to pass by. Anti-Semites spread the vilest untruths about Jewish practices, rumors that were calculated to instill fear and loathing of their Jewish neighbors. Once, when Abram Lipski was a teenager in school, he had a casual gentile acquaintance who rode the tramway with him every day. On the neutral ground of the public transport, the two young men could strike up a conversation and form a friendship that would have otherwise been proscribed in both of their communities. Despite their unusual friendship, however, the gentile friend once asked Abram if it were true that Jews used the blood of murdered gentile babies in their Passover ceremonies! Although taken aback at such a question, it served to show Abram the depth of the gulf which separated Jew and gentile in Poland; there could be no future for a Jew in that country.

The situation of the Jewish community in Poland was one of discrimination and hardship. Entrance into the universities and professions was sharply limited. Although a few wealthy Jews could bribe their way into such institutions, and a few prominent Jews served in the Polish Parliament, most of the Jewish community were merely social outcasts in their own country. They were "strangers in a strange land," an unpopular Jewish minority in a hostile Christian world.

Mathematics and science interested Abram Lipski, and he wanted to use those interests to become an engineer. But engineering was all but closed to Jews who were too poor to pay the bribes, and those few who did qualify for the profession found few clients among the gentile population. Lipski did exceptionally well on the entrance examination for the *Polyteknica Warzawra,* but he was nevertheless denied admission because he was Jewish. With information from an educational clearinghouse, Abram Lipski tried to gain admission to a foreign university. He applied, and was admitted, to the engineering school of the University of Ghent in Belgium.

Belgium was like a breath of fresh air to the young Jewish student who was raised in the bigoted atmosphere of central Poland. Anti-Semitism was, while not exactly nonexistent, very rare among those French- and Flemish-speaking people. Where it was found, anti-Semitism was soon muted by disapproval of other gentiles. There was an air of tolerance in Ghent that was to young Abram's liking—an air of tolerance which became unfortunately rarer the further east one traveled in Europe.

Abram Lipski completed his studies and qualified for the profession of engineering. In 1936, he met and married Tanya Lempert from Bessarabia (in the present-day Soviet Union), the sister of his partner; in 1939, their first child, Raphael Lipski, was born.

The Lipskis lived modestly but without greater hardship than any other young family. Abram's engineering practice was just getting started, but the future looked bright. But in nearby Germany, evil was replacing good in the minds of men. Adolf Hitler, who became Chancellor of Germany in 1933, clamped down ever more tightly on the German Jewish community. Following the cynical 1938 Evian Conference in France, where the world's nations essentially gave Hitler a free hand in regard to the Jews, the lot of the German Jewish community became even more desperate.

The Second World War started on September 1, 1939, with the German invasion of Poland. A few months later, German armies struck westward into France, the Netherlands and Belgium. Once again, virulent anti-Semitism caught up with Abram Lipski.

At first, the Germans did not take any unusual measures towards Belgian Jews. While their kinsmen in the east were herded into walled-off ghettos located in the slum sections of the larger cities, Belgian Jews were left alone—for a while. It was not until several months after the German occupation began that the first measures were taken: on October 28, 1940, all Jews were required to register with the German authorities.

The requirement to register did not seem too onerous to Abram Lipski, so he obeyed the law and properly registered his family. Other families who were not so lucky as the Lipskis were to find out later that registration pinpointed them to the Germans for eventual roundup. The register was later used by coarse

Gestapo raiding parties which rounded up Jews in the middle of the night for deportation to the extermination camps in the east.

Anti-Jewish measures were introduced slowly by the Germans. They knew that Belgians were more likely to protest over such outrages than were the Poles and other Eastern Europeans, so they had to proceed cautiously. Almost imperceptibly, the Germans put increasing pressure on the Jews. Each new restriction was accepted in the belief that it was, in itself, bearable, and in the hope that no further pressure would be brought to bear. Jews were excluded from schools and certain "critical professions," including medicine, law and journalism. Lipski was not directly affected by this edict because engineering was not on the list of banned professions; he was still able to make a living for his small family, and perhaps most important, save money for the day when they had to go underground.

The Jewish population of Ghent was too small to interest the Germans at first. The largest community of Belgian Jews was located in the seaport of Antwerp. In August 1942, disturbing news came from Antwerp. Jews were being rounded up in the middle of the night, and imprisoned in the Dossin Barracks at Malines. When enough were caught to fill a freight train (about 6,000), then the captives were shipped to the extermination camps in Poland. Although the Germans attempted to use the ruse that their destination was agricultural and work colonies in the east, Lipski and others wondered what the real purpose was when they noted that the Germans took not just able-bodied men, but also the women, children, old and sick. Instead of work camps, the captive Jews were sent to their deaths in the extermination camps of Treblinka, Belzec and Sobibor (other death camps were opened a short time later).

The roundups—*rafles*—were usually held late at night when the victims were in bed sleeping. A small caravan of vehicles (a van for the prisoners, a truckload of Gestapo or *Waffen-SS* troops, and a command car) pulled up in front of the house and disgorged armed soldiers. Troops took up positions surrounding the house, while an officer and a small squad went to the front door and pounded on it demanding entrance. The heavy pounding of a jackboot or rifle butt was often the first warning the family received, and by then it was too late. The occupants of the house were given only a few minutes to collect a few personal belongings before they were herded out into the night and onto the vans for transport to the prison barracks.

The reports from Antwerp made Lipski uneasy. Perhaps his eastern European background sensitized him to the danger more than the western Jews who had not known directly the sting of anti-Semitism, or perhaps it is as Peter Hellman suggests: Lipski ". . . caught a whiff of gas." In any event, Lipski took precautions which included preparations for flight and the removal of his wife and son to a small village some distance out of town. Surprisingly, the local German army commander agreed to the move.

From then on, Lipski varied his own schedule to keep from forming a recognizable pattern. He slept each night in a different place in order to reduce the chance of being caught in a *rafle*, should they start in

Ghent as well as Antwerp. One morning, as Abram Lipski was returning home after sleeping out with friends, several neighbors stopped him on the street to warn him that the Gestapo was waiting at his house to arrest him when he returned. From that instant onwards, Abram Lipski and his family became fugitives.

The first problem was to get Tanya and Raphael out of the small village where they were living legally "above ground" as Jews, and into hiding. They were living quite openly, and were registered as Jews with the local German authorities. It would be only a short time before the Germans traced the missing Lipskis to their present home.

Abram and Tanya decided to give up Raphael to the care of others. Although this decision seems difficult to understand from our safe perspective, tragic experience throughout the Holocaust showed that both the children and the parents stood a better chance of survival if split up. Jewish children who did not look too Jewish fared better if they were taken in by gentile families, orphanages or religious orders. The boy's parents sensed this truth, and made arrangements for Raphael to stay with a gentile couple.

Abram and Tanya moved from one refuge to another, never staying in one place too long. There were plenty of blackmailers and informers who would either extort money from hiding Jews in return for silence or turn them in to the Germans to collect the reward. In some European nations, the price of a Jew was a few pounds of bread, some meat or a couple jars of marmalade. Jews in hiding had to be exceedingly careful lest someone spot unusual activity around a hiding place.

They were also forced to move many times because their hosts grew frightened. Where they had initially been willing to take in fugitive Jews, they soon thought better of it and asked the Lipskis to leave. People who had known them a long time suddenly turned out to be weak friends, indeed.

Things fared no better for the three-year-old Raphael. A toddler is an immense burden in the best of times, but the imminent danger of discovery by the Germans just made the pressure all the more severe. The family who agreed to keep Raphael soon became frightened and asked Abram to take him away. It was then that Abram Lipski found himself furtively sneaking through the streets with Raphael bundled in his arms.

It was not easy to find a willing home for a small child. The responsibility, the expense and the danger were almost unsurmountable obstacles for most people. Raphael was placed with first one gentile family, then another. In time, it looked to the Lipskis as though they had run out of places of welcome for their son. It was then that Abram thought of an unlikely candidate: Henriette Chaumat, a young gentile woman whom Abram had met when he first emigrated to Belgium.

Henriette Chaumat was an independent woman who had moved to Ghent at the age of eighteen from her native Paris. She had no husband, no family and seemed like a poor candidate to ask for such help as Abram needed. Nevertheless, Mademoiselle Chaumat agreed. When Abram Lipski asked her to take in his small son, ". . . unlike so many others, she neither gulped nor drew a fearful breath."* So on a cold October night, Abram Lipski retrieved his son at the tramway station and made his way to Mademoiselle Chaumat's apartment.

The next problem was to find a hiding place for themselves. Abram and Tanya had all but exhausted their possibilities, even among friends who a short time earlier had pledged to be available if they ever needed help. Fear is a corrosive thing, and it almost always eroded the courage of those who were initially pleased to offer the fugitive Jewish family a refuge. Abram and Tanya turned to a woman from the poor section of Ghent who once worked in their home as a day servant and charwoman, Hermine Van Assche.

On October 12, 1942, Abram peddled his tandem bicycle to 8 Melkerijstraat in Ghent. He was full of doubts and anxiety as he knocked on the door of his former servant's home. Peter Hellman's description of what happened at that meeting says much about the Righteous Gentiles:

> Hermine herself opened the door and, seeing her fomer employer, began to tremble with what he took for fear. For an instant, he thought that she would simply shut the door on him. *But even as she trembled, she reached out for his arm to bring him into the house.* [emphasis added]

---

*All quotes in this chapter, unless otherwise identified, are from *The Avenue of the Righteous* by Peter Hellman, Atheneum Books, New York, 1980. Used by permission.

Hermine was overjoyed at seeing her old employer and gladly took him in. But before she could make a commitment, however, she had to obtain the permission of the head of the household. Two families shared the small house, and it was the husband of the other family—Pieter Henry—who made all of the decisions for the household. Lipski had arrived early in the morning, and had to wait anyway until evening for a safer traveling time, so he just remained with Hermine until Pieter came home in the late afternoon.

The anxieties of waiting all day for an answer must have been a strain on Abram Lipski. He did not know to whom else he could turn if Pieter Henry denied him refuge. That evening Lipski learned that he had wasted a lot of anxiety. Although he only asked to stay for a short time, Pieter Henry told him that he and Tanya were welcome "for as long as you need." And they were to later learn that Pieter Henry was not a man to extend spurious offers of aid, or to renege if he became fearful.

Lipski returned to the Henry-Van Assche home later that night with Tanya. He discovered still another measure of the Henry family. When Pieter called the Lipskis "honored guests," he meant it. The attic room that would serve Abram and Tanya as their *mellina* (hiding place) was not cleared out, nor was it habitable and secure. Pieter Henry gave the Lipskis his own master bedroom for several days until the camouflaged *mellina* was ready. Pieter brushed aside Lipski's embarrassed objections and insisted that they accept the best bedroom in the house. According to Hellman's account, Lipski learned ". . . that in the matter of simple decency, men could vault as high as they slither low. They seemed to do either, moreover, with equal unexpectedness and for equally little reason."

Some Jews were able to live above ground in Belgium. Those who did not look Jewish, and did not have Abram Lipski's East European accent, were able to pose as Christians. Just as in nearby France, the underground resistance operated printing plants to forge gentile documents. A happy circumstance for Jews in the vicinity of Ghent was that the city hall in a nearby town had burned down a few years before the war, taking with it all of the records that could be used to cross-check faked papers: there were no records to contradict the forged documents. The Lipskis had to live completely underground, however, because their accents marked them as foreigners.

The hiding place in the Henry attic had to be prepared so that no trace of their existence could be detected from without or within the house. The two large attic windows had to be completely blacked out. If even the dimmest light glowed from those windows, then a passer-by or neighbor could guess that someone was hiding in the attic.

Sound had to be muffled. If any visitor heard unexplained moving about upstairs, there was the possibility that their next stop after leaving the Henry home would be Gestapo headquarters. The Lipskis even had to hide from the six-year-old child of one of the couples: old enough to know, but not old enough to know better than to talk about the people in the attic.

A bell alarm system was rigged to permit communication between downstairs and the attic. If the bell rang once, the Lipskis went downstairs immediately; if twice, they could move about and go downstairs if they pleased; if three times, they were to remain absolutely silent and still. A trapdoor leading from the attic to the roof provided an escape route if the Germans came. The Lipskis went out on a trial run one night, and were probably glad after liberation that they never had to scurry across those high roofs to safety!

Although there were anxious moments, no one ever discovered Abram and Tanya Lipski. Once, when a friend boasted to Pieter Henry that Jews were hiding in his home, Henry replied that he would never be so brave as to take in fugitive Jews. Throughout Europe, prideful indiscretions like that of Henry's friend cost the lives of many hiding Jews—and their hosts.

Abram fared better than many hiding Jews because he was able to make a modest living while in hiding. One of his gentile clients from before the war, a Christian who owned a factory, kept him furnished with work for much of the two years of his life underground. Abram could work in the attic and deliver the drawings after dark—preferably on nights when the weather was bad enough to keep German patrols under shelter.

The problems faced by Mademoiselle Chaumat with young Raphael were different than the problem of hiding adults. A young child had to live in the open because it was impossible to guarantee the child's silence at critical times. At the same time, however, a three-year-old child is already accustomed to his name and speaks well enough to give away the secret under interrogation. The first several months, then, were spent indoors teaching Raphael a new name and new identity.

That new identity took a little thought. How does a single woman suddenly produce a three-year-old child when all of her friends knew that she had never been pregnant? At first, Raphael was an "orphaned nephew," but that ruse could not last too long. For the sake of security, Mademoiselle Chaumat moved to an apartment in a small village out of town where they were not known. They lived in that apartment for a while, until Raphael was recognized. They moved to still another small village, about twenty minutes outside of Ghent, and remained there until liberation in 1944.

Henriette Chaumat was an attractive woman, so it was natural that she had male friends. Her constant companion in those years was a doctor from Ghent. Many of the gossips in the village drew the conclusion that Raphael was a "love child" from that relationship, so they tended to purse a sly smile whenever Mademoiselle Chaumat and Raphael passed by. Far from being angered at such a suggestion, Mademoiselle Chaumat found it helpful to have the child identified as illegitimate, for the rumor squelched other inquiries into the child's origins.

Allied armies invaded Hitler's *Festung Europa* (Fortess Europe) on June 6, 1944, with landings at Normandy in France. All of Europe followed the progress of the Allied armies on BBC, despite the fact that listening to enemy broadcasts in Nazi-occupied Europe was a crime punishable with death or a trip to the concentration camps. On September 6, 1944, the American and British armies liberated Brussels and

Ghent, Belgium: the Lipskis were free—they had survived the Holocaust.

Readjustment was not easy, especially for the child Raphael, who by that time had grown attached to Henriette Chaumat. But Abram and Tanya were not disappointed, for little Raphael easily reverted to his old identity. Perhaps we do not give children as much credit as they deserve. As a test, during the time Raphael lived with Mademoiselle Chaumat, Abram and Tanya visited the apartment. The boy was distant and did not seem to recognize his parents. But once the need for the charade was over, he had no difficulty recognizing mama and papa.

Some years later, the sons of Raphael Lipski—Abram and Tanya's grandsons—planted carob trees on the Avenue of the Righteous at Yad Vashem in Jerusalem for the Henry family and for Henriette Chaumat.

10
Sietske Postma

Early one June morning in 1942, a practical nurse named Nurit Hegd crept out of her dormitory in Amsterdam's Nederland-Israelitsch Hospital. The sleepy guard noticed her, but said nothing as the twenty-two-year-old Jewish woman left the building. The Germans had started rounding up Jews only a few months before, again using the lie that they were being sent to work colonies in the east. The captives were held for a while at the transit barracks in the Westerbork Concentration Camp near Amsterdam and then shipped by railroad to the infamous murder camp Auschwitz. Most of the Dutch Jews sent to the camp were murdered in the gas chambers within a few days of their arrival, often on the very same day.

Nurit had worked previously as a teletypewriter operator in the Dutch post office, but was dismissed when German edict banned Jews from the civil service. The government nevertheless managed to continue her salary for a while, but she eventually had to find another job. Hospitals had been safe havens from

Gestapo raids, so she joined the Nederland-Israelitsch Hospital as a nurse. The safety of the hospital was to be short-lived. Jewish deportation quotas had not been met, so Adolf Eichmann ordered that hospitals and mental institutions be raided. Every morning the guard saw several frightened young women slip out to the comparative security of the underground life.

Nurit made her way to the central train station where she waited at the appointed spot between two postal deposit boxes. Another nurse had slipped out fifteen minutes earlier, and was already waiting for their contact from the Dutch Underground Resistance. They followed the woman from the Resistance onto a train that was bound northward to Leeuwarden, the provincial capital of Friesland. Acting as if they did not know their guide, Nurit and the other woman entered a compartment and, in an act of youthful high adventure, sat down next to a pair of uniformed Dutch SS soldiers.

After lunching in Leeuwarden at the dining room of the Hotel Organje, Nurit boarded a bus for the small village of Ferwerd. That small Friesian village of three thousand was a community of craftsmen and farmers who practiced strict brands of Lutheran and Dutch Reform Protestantism. The people of the region around Ferwerd closely adhere to what German sociologist Max Weber once called "the Protestant work ethic." The farms and businesses were profitably run, and the town and its homes were perpetually clean and well kept even in hard war times. Even though the cities of the Netherlands were on the brink of starvation in those years, the agricultural bounty of Friesland made hunger rare in that rural province.

Friesland was a good place to hide Jews, especially the more ethnic-looking Sephardic Jews that were once the very core of the Dutch Jewish community. The Germans did not see fit to establish a large military presence in sparsely settled Friesland. In Ferwerd, which was but an hour's drive from the German border, the only German authority was an SS man stationed in a neighboring village. That specimen of Hitler's elite made his patrols on a bicycle because his post was not deemed important enough for an automobile or motorcycle. There was always plenty of warning when he was coming, for the kids would shout "Mustache is coming!" Most of the young men would then slip into hiding to avoid being drafted into Hitler's Volunteer Labor Brigade.

When Nurit stepped off the bus in Ferwerd she was met by the village doctor. The stern-faced old physician had few words for her. He told her to follow him down the street at a discreet distance, and to knock on the door of the house that would be immediately on her left when the doctor signaled by stopping to look at his pocket watch.

When the doctor stopped at a small house near the town square, Nurit went up to its door and knocked. The door was opened by Sietske Postma, the daughter of the family.

"My name is Franciska Slujk" (a pseudonym), said Nurit ". . . I don't have any money . . . today is my birthday."

"My name is Sietske Postma . . . in this house you

don't need any money" said the young woman who greeted her.

Although she was not sure why she blurted out the fact that it was her birthday, "Franciska" (nee Nurit) had very good reasons for volunteering the information concerning her poverty. There were many in Holland (and all other occupied countries) who offered aid to fleeing Jews only in consideration of payment. One factor that distinguishes the Righteous Gentiles from others who aided Jews was that no money or other material consideration was demanded. Many thousands of Jews had to bribe their way to safety or an all-too-shaky security.

Those who lacked gold or currency to pay their benefactors were often practically enslaved. On many cold Friesian farms, urban Jews did unaccustomed manual labor in the fields from sunup to sundown. The cost of haven on an isolated gentile farm was near slavery, and the hapless Jews had little power to alter their situation. After all, if they objected too loudly, their hosts could demand that they leave.

But the Postma family was "truly remarkable." When Nurit tried to help in the kitchen, or sweep out the wood chips from Djoerd Postma's carpentry shop, they would refuse to permit it. They let her know in no uncertain terms that she was a guest, not a maid. It would be a long time before the Postmas would let Nurit help with the chores, until it was absolutely clear to her that working was not a condition of the aid offered. Such was frequently true of the Righteous Gentiles.

The kindness of the Postmas was shown in many

little ways. When Nurit needed shoes, for example, her gentile "sister" Sietske gave up a precious ration coupon for a pair of shoes so that Nurit could have a new pair. Nurit had fled Amsterdam in the heat of summer, with only a small supply of light clothing. When fall came and the Germans were still undefeated, it became necessary to provide Nurit with a winter coat. Sietske gave her own coat to Nurit, and then acquired some material to make an inferior but serviceable coat for herself.

Nurit Hegd witnessed in the Postmas a simple kind of religious faith. Never very religious herself—she came from a nonpracticing family of nearly assimilated Jews—she marveled at the piety of the Postma family; she was also threatened by it, even though none of the Postmas pressured her over religious matters. Nurit found herself living with a family that gathered three times a day for meals, Bible readings by the father, and prayer done with clasped hands around a table. She also had to attend services at the Dutch Reformed Church with her adoptive family. But it was not out of religious feeling, only a simple matter of security. She was posing as a distant relative, for there were informers in the area, and it would be suspicious if she remained at home when the family went to church. So the secularized Jewish girl from Amsterdam wound up sitting in a rural Protestant church raising her voice in singing the hymns.

Never previously a Zionist, the war made her an ardent supporter of the movement to establish a Jewish state in Palestine. Where she had previously ignored those who had a passion for Palestine, she was now a convinced Zionist. Eventually she would settle in Israel.

In time, her Zionism and the pressures of living a pseudo-Christian life in a hostile world that wanted to murder her caused her to resent this Jesus that her hosts prayed to so regularly. Her attitude may seem lamentable to us who live in comparative safety, but very clearly illustrates the perceptions of Jews even today. Those Jews who lived in Europe over the centuries had long, sad experiences with men who invoked the name of Jesus. Not knowing Christ himself, but only supposed followers of Christ, has exacted a terrible toll among Jews. Their misperceptions are, unfortunately, fairly arrived at through a long chain of terrifying experiences. All too often, while evil men among us slaughtered Jews, the "righteous" stood by and let them!

11

The Unrighteous Gentiles

The large majority of gentiles in Europe, believers and nonbelievers alike, turned their eyes and hearts away from the Jews as they were being murdered. For most, the motive was fear—fear of reprisal, fear of death itself. The Nazis executed or sent to concentration camps those gentiles who aided Jews, so one can see how a Christian man might have had cause for concern when a Jew asked for help. There were others, including leaders of the churches, whose actions or refusal to take action resulted in Jewish casualties. In some cases, it was fear that motivated them, while in others it was the anti-Semitism implicit in certain popular (but nonetheless false) Christian teachings. In this chapter, we will take a brief look at some areas that are in contrast to the other stories in this book; it is a necessary negative look. We will see how the governments of the Western world closed their borders to Jewish emigration. We will also see how the Church responded as a whole, despite the nobility of individual heroes and heroines; and by way of a lesson, we shall also see what Hitler had planned for the church after he was finished with the Jews.

When the Nations Slammed Their Doors

A fateful conference was held on January 20, 1942, at a villa in the Berlin suburb of Am Grossen Wansee. Assembled under the chairmanship of SS Lieutenant General Reinhard Heydrich were the Deputies and Secretaries—the second-echelon managers—of certain key agencies of the German government: foreign ministry, Interior, Justice, Gestapo, the *Reichs-chancellory,* the Four-Year Economic Plan, and the Civil Administration of the Occupied Territories of the East. The minutes of the Wansee Conference were taken by a previously unknown SS bureaucrat named Adolf Eichmann. "Even now," claimed General Heydrich, "practical experience is being gathered in the east that is of major significance in view of the coming *Final Solution of the Jewish Question."*

Thus were the functionaries of Hitler's death engine told of what had been termed the most significant decision since Pontius Pilate's: the attempted complete extermination of world Jewry!

The "experience" referred to by SS General Heydrich was being gathered on the blood-drenched eastern front where 3,000 specially selected SS men, who were formed into four Special Action Forces, were systematically flushing out and murdering the Jews of Russia and other former Soviet territories taken by the German army. By the time of the Wansee Conference, over 90 percent of the Jews who were trapped in the

German-occupied area east of the Soviet border had been killed—most of them shot by SS firing squads.

Neither the Wansee Conference nor the murders of the Russian Jews, however, was the opening of the Holocaust; the actual beginnings are found several years earlier, in 1938. Historians agree that 1938 was a grim turning point for German Jews, and was the last year in which there were any signs of organized Jewish community life in Germany.

Nazi Foreign Minister Joachim von Ribbontrop also saw 1938 as a decisive turning point for the Nazis and their Jewish victims. In a telegram that he sent to all German diplomatic and consular offices abroad in January 1939, he stated: "It is not by chance that 1938, the year of our destiny, saw a *major step towards the solution of the Jewish problem"* (italics added). Did the world know of the impending disaster facing Europe's Jewish population? Had there been any signs of Hitler's intent prior to the start of the killing? What did the nations of the world do about the situation? These questions and others scream out for answers, yet only recently have historians come to grips with the problem. The awful truth is that there were few Good Samaritans among the nations of the world during the seven years of the Holocaust. Most of the world just walked by the stricken Israelites on the other side of the road—we were the Pharisees of the biblical story!

By 1938, the Jews of Germany had suffered five years of increasingly harsh persecution at the hands of the Nazis. The Nuremburg Laws of 1935 sealed into law the most vile Nazi prejudices. In 1938, thirty-two nations gathered at Evian, France, to discuss the plight of the German Jews in an international conference that was called by President Roosevelt of the United States.

Two hundred delegates, observers and members of the press gathered at the Hotel Royal in Evian, a pleasant little resort spa on the French side of Lake Geneva. The conference lasted from July 6 to July 14, 1938. The nations of Czechoslovakia and the USSR were not represented at the conference, and Mussolini's Fascist government of Italy declined to send a representative. The Eastern European nations of Poland, Hungary, and Romania merely sent observers whose only assignment was to explore ways to be rid of their own native Jewish populations. Germany sent no official delegation, but did contemptuously permit representatives of the German and Austrian Jewish communities to attend. Golda Meir, future Prime Minister of the then-nonexistent nation of Israel, came from Palestine to attend.

From the very opening of the conference, the proceedings were tinged with cynicism and evasions. The World Jewish Committee, which represented seven million Jews worldwide, was allowed only five minutes to present its case. The German and Austrian Jewish delegations, being merely observers, were not allowed to speak at all and were required to submit only written comments.

One by one, the delegates of thirty-two sovereign nations arose to speak. Each one deplored the plight of Germany's Jews, but alas, could offer no help whatever: ". . . perhaps one of the other nations . . .?" Only the Dominican Republic offered to increase their quota of Jewish immigrants. That Carribean island nation was in desperate need of agricultural "pioneers," and was willing to give a few urbanized Jews from Germany the opportunity to emigrate. The pattern of the conference was visible as early as the third day. On July 8, 1938, the *New York Herald Tribune* could announce in bold headlines: "POWERS SLAM DOOR AGAINST GERMAN JEWS."

The most cynical statement of the conference came on the last day, July 14. Not wishing to appear hardened against the Jews, the delegates announced that they encouraged emigration, but that ". . . the countries of asylum are not willing to undertake any obligations toward financing involuntary immigration." Since Hitler's government permitted Jews to take no more than $5 in cash and none of their personal property when they emigrated, this statement was tantamount to shutting the door in the faces of the hapless Jews. In the years that followed, the number of Jews who escaped from Germany dropped to 27,000— a mere trickle, a number that is less than a few hours' killing at Auschwitz! In fact, all of the German Jewish emigration to the United States from 1933 until 1938 was less than two days' killing in the gas chambers of that one death camp.

The Nazis were quick to gloat over the results of the Evian Conference. The headline of the Nazi newspaper *Reichswart* crowed: "JEWS FOR SALE—WHO WANTS THEM? NO ONE." The Gestapo newspaper *Schwarzkorp* boastfully proclaimed: "No power on earth can hinder us, we will now bring the Jewish question to its totalitarian solution." Hitler, ever consistent to his earliest statements, told the South

African Minister of Defense: "We shall solve the Jewish problem in the immediate future . . . *the Jews will disappear."*

The start of the Holocaust can be dated from the Evian Conference. The nations of the world effectively slammed shut their national frontiers on the Jews, thereby sending Hitler a signal that he was free to proceed with the planned liquidation. In the months that followed Evian, the noose tightened ever more around the necks of Germany's Jews.

One of the first post-Evian insults by the Germans was the so-called "Globke Decree," issued on August 17, 1938, only a month after the conclusion of the conference. By this decree, Jews were humiliated even further by stripping them of their given names. Under the terms of the Globke decree, all Jewish males were required to adopt "Israel" as their first name, and all Jewish females were renamed "Sara."

The Swiss government, perhaps nervously mindful of their long border with Germany, requested that the German government mark the passports of all Jews with some sort of distinguishing symbol. The Germans obliged by marking the passports of all Jews with a large red letter "J." Escaping Jews could then be distinguished from vacationing non-Jews—and quickly returned to Germany whence they came.

South American countries, some of which had large pro-Nazi German expatriate populations, ruthlessly closed their doors to the Jews. Most of them adopted extremely restrictive Jewish immigration laws that read as if they had been drafted in Josef Goebbels's propaganda ministry.

The attitude of the world community is summed up in a memo on the Evian Conference that was sent in October 1938 to the German Foreign Minister by the French government: "None of the states would dispute the absolute right of the German government to take with regard to certain of its citizens such measures as are within its sovereign powers." In other words, do as you please, Germany; we, the "righteous" of the world, will not interfere.

Kristalnacht

In what historian Robert G.L. Waite called a "jarring accident of chronology," the first widespread, organized violence against the Jews took place on the night of November 9-10, 1938—Martin Luther's birthday anniversary! *Kristalnacht* ("Crystal Night" in English) is named for the mountains of broken glass from Jewish synagogues, businesses and homes that were attacked that night. Nazi gangs went on a spontaneous binge of murder and violence that was orchestrated by the Gestapo and Goebbels' Ministry of Propaganda and Enlightenment.

Kristalnacht was precipitated by the singular act of a seventeen-year-old Jewish boy in Paris. Herschell Grynspan was distraught over the plight of his parents who, along with thousands of other Polish Jews who resided in Germany, were expelled from the Third Reich. The deportees were herded at bayonet point across the border into Poland, even though the Polish government had refused them entry. The 17,000 people lived in makeshift camps in no man's land between the two frontiers with inadequate food, heat and sanitation.

The upset young Grynspan bought a small-caliber pistol, walked into the German Embassy in Paris, and asked to see the Ambassador, but was referred instead to the Third Secretary. When Secretary vom Rath admitted Grynspan to his office, the youngster pulled out the pistol and emptied its contents into vom Rath's body. Goebbels had been looking for an incident to hang on the Jews, so he used the vom Rath murder to whip up public furor over the supposed "World Jewish Conspiracy" who, he alleged, had sent Grynspan on his deadly mission.

German police were conspicuously absent on the Night of Broken Glass, *Kristalnacht.* They kept out of the way while Nazi storm troopers went on a rampage. Thirty-six Jews were murdered that night, and scores of synagogues were burned to the ground. Thousands of Jews were arrested and sent to the concentration camps: 10,911 to Dachau near Munich, 9,845 to Buchenwald and 9,000 to Sachsenhaussen. The world reaction to *Kristalnacht* was restrained outrage.

Two months after *Kristalnacht,* Adolf Hitler told Czechoslovakian Foreign Minister Chvalkovsky: "We are going to destroy the Jews . . . the day of reckoning has come!" Nine days later, on January 30, 1939, Hitler used his speech commemorating the sixth anniversary of his ascension to power to tell the world: "In a New World, the Jewish race in Europe will be destroyed." In the years that followed, Hitler very nearly carried out that threat!

Where Was the Church?

In a twisted and almost demonic way, the Church abetted Hitler's slaughter of the Jewish people. None of the major factions of Christianity can flee their guilt over the Holocaust. Neither Protestant nor Roman Catholic nor Eastern Orthodox churches can say that their branch of Christendom had nothing to do with the ultimate fate of the 6,000,000 dead. Even the evangelical Confessional Church, which was formed by Pastor Niemoeller and others in response to Nazism, was not above the need for repentance after the war.

The organized churches were guilty of both sins of commission and omission. In many instances, the churches remained silent in the face of Nazi outrages. In other cases, the churches actively aided and supported the Nazis. In still other cases, the churches failed to counter erroneous teachings that eventually led to easy acceptance of Nazi doctrine.

Finally, the official church bodies failed to provide aid and rescue for Jewish victims who were trying to escape the Nazi dragnet. When the pastor Trocmé in France decided to take in refugees, for example, his Superintendent chastised him for his charity. It was viewed as too dangerous to aid the contemptible Jews. With notable exceptions, the policy of the Church was to remain inappropriately neutral.

The state of the Church during that era is perhaps best illustrated by its reaction to *Kristalnacht* (November 9-10, 1938) when German storm troopers went on the rampage killing Jews, burning synagogues and vandalizing Jewish homes and businesses.

Thousands of Jews were arrested and sent to concentration camps during that night, but only one major Christian leader raised a vigorous public protest against the outrage: Dietrich Bonhoeffer. Of that night, Bonhoeffer said: "Only he who cries in protest on behalf of the Jews has a right to sing the Gregorian chant." Bonhoeffer's cries of protest were lonely, for no other leading churchman spoke out!

There is no guarantee that vigorous Christian protest would have stopped Hitler. Given Hitler's own personality and the demonic influences over him, it is unlikely that he would have been successfully swayed by the protests of the churchmen whom he despised so much. The Holocaust would have still occurred, but probably with a much lower death toll. Individual Christians, and small groups working together outside the framework of the institutional church, could have been spurred on by their leaders to act out of Christian love towards their Jewish neighbors. How many more "Righteous Gentiles" would have been emboldened to action by the heroic actions of their leaders? We will never know.

Understanding the moral treason of churchmen requires knowledge of the doctrinal state of much of the church in Europe during the first four decades of this century. The satanic influences of the German and other theologians and philosophers of the nineteenth century had grown to a point where Scripture was regarded by many as just a collection of Jewish poems and historical anecdotal data of doubtful accuracy; Christ was demoted to the position of a "great moral teacher" if He existed at all, or a fictional composite of several great moral teachers if He did not; God, if any, was dead. Sin was explained away as naturally caused aberrations by the rising new profession of psychology, and the entire basis of Christian ethics was subverted on a humanist altar. A Christian church which no longer believed itself subject to God's will was ill-equipped to cope with a satanic event the magnitude of the Holocaust. While church leaders often laid profound ethical foundations for their de-Christified Christianity, they neatly excised the very heart of Christian ethics: obedience to God. The hollow shell that remained found it too easy to adapt to changing conditions and thereby took on the role of a silently disapproving spectator of the destruction of Jewry. Of course, with righteous hindsight we can now learn that silent disapproval of sin is the same as tacit approval.

It is interesting to note that Satan managed to devitalize the churches with generations of liberal theology and agnostic, if not outright atheist, churchmen at exactly the moment in history when he was about to launch his most hellish attack on the Chosen People. Satan used man's own pride in his intellectual achievement to remove the churches from his path.

It is probably the lack of Christian ethics firmly embedded in sound, fundamental doctrine that led to the Holocaust. Men who do not know, or refuse to accept, Holy Scripture as the Word of God would not know how to overcome their fear of Satan's minions with the power of the Word.

Fortunately for the victims of Hitler, there were local and regional exceptions to the rule governing church behavior. Many times, local pastors and other leaders resisted the Nazis and aided the Jews in a state of disobedience to their church superiors. People like Mother Maria, Father Pierre Chaillet (a Roman Catholic priest in Lyon, France) and Andre Trocmé fully understood their ethical responsibilities toward the Jewish refugees who came their way. These people risked death (Mother Maria was executed at Ravensbrueck) to hide Jews and spirit them away to safety. It was primarily through people like them that God chose to save the ever present remnant of Israel—again.

The ethical precepts that most nominal Christians operate under are the Ten Commandments. It is believed that under these commandments, a person sins by actively breaking one of the rules. But the saints who became the lifeline for the Jews realized a broader implication of the greatest commandment (Matt. 22:36-40) was that passively watching another person do evil to a helpless victim was the same as doing that evil oneself—even if aiding the victim means risking one's life, silence is sin.

The Church the world over is split into denominations, factions and splinter groups that rarely have anything to do with each other except to throw mud. Doctrinal, liturgical and mere procedural disputes have caused antagonism among Christians that comforts only Satan. Sometimes, our differences are so acute that no communication at all is possible. Such was also true of the church in Europe prior to World War II. In France, the historical split between Roman Catholics and the Protestants was so complete that Fr. Chaillet's Christian Witness group in Lyon and Pastor Trocme's people in the village of Le-Chambon-sur-Lignon only 100 miles away were unaware of each other for much of the war.

The Church's sins of omission were apparently motivated by fear of reprisal, lubricated by decades of liberal encroachment. The sins of commission, however, were almost universally the result of Church anti-Semitism. The European church (and also the American . . . lest we become haughty and proud) exhibited anti-Semitic behavior that ranged from mild contempt for the Jewish people to outright Jew-hatred.

For the hapless Jewish refugee fleeing from Nazi terror there was little practical difference between the two forms of anti-Semitism! Only when coupled with violent or treacherous acts was outright hatred for the Jews worse than the passive but nonetheless malignant neglect of those who were merely contemptuous of the Jews.

The Church's neglect of the Jewish people cannot be laid to mere ignorance of the situation, because knowledge of Hitler's Final Solution was too wide-spread. The Roman Catholic hierarchy was especially well informed on events in Eastern Europe. According to historian Walter Laqueur, the Vatican was among the first to know that deportation meant death for the Jews. Evidence exists that the Vatican was aware of these events only a few weeks after the Wansee Conference of January, 1942.

The Vatican's sources involved both regular and irregular channels of communications. The regular channels consisted of diplomatic offices of the Vatican, Papal Nuncios and official church travelers. Irregular sources included priests ranked from the lowest novice in the local parish churhces all the way up to Cardinals and Archbishops, nuns and monks in the religious orders, and the millions of rank-and-file Catholics who ardently believe in their church. These people readily received and fed information and eyewitness accounts to Vatican officials. Those officials enjoyed diplomatic immunity even in Nazi-occupied Europe, a fact that is of no little importance.

Nazi Attitude Toward the Church

The Church has enjoyed varying degrees of success in the different European countries. In some nations, the Church enjoyed practically no respect and had a following to match. In those countries, the Nazis could safely ignore the church, and did. While contemptuous of all churches, Hitler was most contemptuous of the lukewarm and he was fond of misquoting the words of Revelation concerning the Laodicean church (Rev. 3:14-17).

Where the Church was well regarded, the Nazis had to be wary of its power and influence. Thus Hitler had to at least tolerate the Roman Catholic church because of its immense popularity in France and in some of the nations of Eastern Europe. An exception was Poland, where the Roman Catholic Church enjoys immense popularity, but German priorities were sufficiently great to risk the wrath of the church. While Heinrich Himmler advocated the public execution of Pope Pius XII, Hitler was a lot more pragmatic. He allowed those clerics who did not actively oppose him to remain in their pulpits.

Most of the top Nazis shared Himmler's poor regard for the Church. Those who did not openly hate the Church were at least contemptuous of it. There was little to fear from the lukewarm church, so the SS could continue its murderous plans. It can be demonstrated convincingly that even the top Nazis feared public exposure of the Final Solution and backed off wherever public officials opposed them.

Hermann Rauschning recorded Hitler's views on the Church prior to 1934. In his dinner conversations, Hitler often expounded on the Protestant and Roman Catholic churches. Hitler respected the power and organization of the Roman Catholic Church, and indeed formed the Nazi Party along the lines of the church; the SS was formed along the lines of the Jesuits. Hitler believed that "Providence" fated him to be raised a Catholic "for only a Catholic knows the weaknesses of the church." He believed that Germany's first Chancellor, Prince Otto von Bismarck, was foolish in his relationship with the Roman Catholic Church. According to Hitler: "Bismarck was a fool. In other words, he was a Protestant. Protestants don't know what a church is."

German Protestants eagerly sought to use Nazism as a vehicle to become the dominant church in the *Reich,* a hope from which they were rudely disabused. The Protestants who were militantly anti-Rome wanted to become under the Nazis a united, evangelical German national church in which the Roman Catholics would be either expelled altogether or occupy a severely subordinate role at best. Hitler's views on the Protestants, again provided to us by Rauschning, are summed up by one of his dinner statements: "The Protestants haven't the faintest conception of a church. You can do anything you like with them—they will submit. These pastors are used to cares and worries . . . they learnt them from their squires. The parsons, when they were invited to the Sunday roast goose, had their place at the foot of the table amongst the children and tutors. It was even an honor that they were not asked to sit at the servant's table. They are insignificant little people, submissive as dogs, and they sweat with embarrassment when you talk to them. They have neither a religion that they can take seriously nor a great position to defend like Rome." Hitler felt that Protestant pastors would go along with anything that he demanded of them because their main concern was worry over the security of their old-age pensions. What a sorry state the evangelical churches had come to if a man as politically astute as Adolf Hitler could only hold them in utter contempt. I suspect that the reason for the state of affairs lies in weak doctrine and the lukewarm responses that such produces.

Hitler's Plans for the Church and Religion

Adolf Hitler courted the churches when it suited his purposes, and then just as glibly abandoned them to pursue his own ends. Hitler actively opposed the churches and the Gospel of Jesus Christ. For him, there was no compromise possible . . . the church had to go.

Hitler's eventual plans for the Church after (he supposed) winning the war are shown by a conversation between *Reichsfuehrer-SS* Heinrich Himmler and his personal physician, Dr. Felix Kersten. Himmler had his personal railroad car parked on a siding in France while waiting for Hitler to call for him. Kersten had been required to make the trip in case Himmler's ailment returned, so he had little to do except wander about. On this occasion he noticed that *Himmler's personal library contained only religious books.* Perplexed, he confronted Himmler with the paradox, asking whether or not religion and Nazism were antithetical. Himmler replied that Hitler had ordered him to prepare the basic doctrines of a great German religion that would be imposed on all of Europe. The religion of the Nazi New Age would be a blend of ancient Germanic paganism, Eastern mysticism and a bastardized Christianity in which Hitler would take the place of Christ. The real Christian Church would be suppressed, and eventually would be totally discarded. A thousand years later, only Hitler's religion would remain.

Oddly, the Church had been quick in the past to cry out against heresies, but to the Nazi heresy they were quiet. It is not that they were unaware of Hitler's intentions! Even in the 1920's Hitler was fond of comparing himself favorably with Christ, and as early as 1934 German school children were required to recite prayers thanking their *Fuehrer* rather than God for the benefits they received.

Conclusion

Satan severely challenged all factions of the Church during the Holocaust, and they were found wanting. Missing were the love which Christ taught, the desire to fight against sin, and the doctrinal strength to oppose massive evil. The Holocaust has given the Church, the organized Body of Christ, an almost unique opportunity to repent and return to that first love which the first-century Christians knew. The modern nation of Israel should have no firmer friends than Christians who know what the cancer of anti-Semitism engenders.

12
Epilogue

Jewish attitudes towards the Church perplex many Christians. We see ourselves in a kindly light, and cannot perceive even a single shred of malice in our hearts towards the Jewish people. Our explanation for their attitude usually takes the form of a vague statement about "rejecting Jesus Christ." We often blame an alleged spiritual blindness of the Jews for their almost unanimous rejection of Christian evangelism.

Yet in increasing numbers today, there are Jews recognizing the Messiah. But their confession of faith is not without personal cost. Many of our Jewish neighbors have serious doubts about Jewish converts to Christianity; the very word "convert" is anathema. It seems to them that any convert is little more than a hypocrite, or at best an enigmatic puzzle. It is difficult for them to understand the Jew who follows Jesus. A Jew who converts to Christianity will be ostracized by family and friends alike, and may even be cast out of the familiar culture in which he or she grew up. Former friends will consider the Hebrew Christian to be *meshumed,* a traitor who betrayed his people, his heritage and the blood of countless Jewish martyrs.

A person can remain "Jewish" despite major differences in religious outlook. An atheist, an agnostic or even the follower of obscure Eastern religious cults can remain "Jewish" in the eyes of his community, but if the Jew becomes a *Christian,* then he or she is no longer considered Jewish! A letter published in *Christian Life* in early 1984 reaffirmed that opinion, regarding Jews who become Christians as "apples trying to be oranges." The family of such a Jew may cast him out and some have even been known to say *Kaddish* (a funeral prayer for the dead) for members of the family who have accepted Messiah Jesus.

Unfortunately, the other part of the problem—and no little insignificant part at that—is sin of the Church and some of its otherwise most righteous members. Many times throughout its history, the Church has bared its collective teeth at the Jews and manifest satanic hatred of God's Chosen People through vile teaching from the pulpit, vicious laws promulgated by supposedly Christian governments, and both subtle and virulent forms of that most malignant of spiritual tumors: anti-Semitism.

The Jews cannot easily perceive the real Christianity. Neither can they perceive the real Jesus, because they must see him through the filter of the Church—and a dark and murky filter it has sometimes been. The Jewish attitude towards Jesus is intimately related to their practical experiences with the professed followers of Jesus—the Church. "By their fruits ye shall know them," and in all too many cases the fruits of the Church seen by Jews have been persecution, slander and murder. This unfortunate cultural identification, although mandated by historical imperative, tends to place our Savior in a very bad light among the Jewish communities. Prominent Jews have frequently referred to Jesus as a luminary (as did Albert Einstein), or a great teacher, while at the same time refusing to identify Him as their long-awaited Messiah. The reasons for this situation are less spiritual blindness than a reaction to the long history of Christian persecution of the Jewish people.

It is indeed one of the most monumental contradictions of history that *the main obstacle standing between Jesus Christ and His own people Israel is the Church!* When you are tempted to accuse the Jewish people of having scales over their eyes, keep in mind while boasting of your spirituality that the glue that holds those scales so firmly in place is *you.*

From what evil soil does this bitter root spring? Why does the Jew fail to see the differences between the Crusader who raped his great-great-great-grandmother, or the soldiers of the Grand Inquisitor who tortured his great-grandfather on the king's rack, or the Nazi who gassed his grandfather . . . and the well-scrubbed Christian who preaches the Gospel to his people. Some Jewish leaders believe "sooner lose one to Hitler than to the Christians." For the answers to these questions we must examine the long and sometimes sordid history of relations between Christians and Jews.

The Jews are the most persecuted people in all of

history. Their story goes back nearly 6,000 years, and that story has been one of periodic catastrophe, of which the Holocaust is but the most recent example. Israel is such an ancient people that their history has spanned four great world empires. At a time when Rome was nothing more than a collection of late-Bronze Age mud huts along the Tiber Riber, the glory of King Solomon's Temple had come and gone—and the people of Israel were captives in Babylon. Persecution and domination by foreign rulers has been their lot ever since, and their holy city Jerusalem was under gentile domination for two millenia.

The early history of the Church is essentially a page from Jewish history, and both branches of God's olive tree were cruelly persecuted by the Romans. For the first several centuries, certainly the first century, there was a great deal of communication between gentile and Jewish believers in Jesus. It was not until well after the Church gained political power as the official religion of the Roman Empire that significant persecution of the Jews became possible. Although certain gentile Christian leaders of the second and third centuries routinely condemned the Jews, it was only after Christians assumed political power that the Jews suffered extensively at the hands of Christians.

The Church in the Middle Ages began to teach that the Jews were "Christ Killers," and thus collectively guilty of deicide (killing God). We found it convenient to remember that Judas Iscariot and High Priest Caiaphas were Jews, while forgetting that Jesus and all of the disciples were Jews. It became easy to forget that it was gentile hands—not Jewish—that nailed Jesus to the cross; gentile hands in the service of the very government which the Church had only so recently joined.

During the medieval period, mobs rallying under the banner of Christ frequently attacked Jewish communities and slaughtered the people. Christian holidays—the word means "holy days"—became an especially fearsome time for the Jewish populations of Christian Europe because unruly gangs used the holidays as a convenient excuse to mutilate a few Jews. Holy Week, encompassing Good Friday and Easter Sunday, was especially a time of dread for the Jews because it was the time of the year when Christians were most likely to dredge up the old lie of "Christ Killer." Jewish holidays were also a fearsome time because Christian marauders often selected such times for their attacks. The reason was that Jews would be in their homes or synagogues on the holidays, making the attack all the more successful.

Despite the fact that Christ preached a doctrine of forgiveness, and that God himself in the Old Testament period only visited the sins of the fathers unto the third or fourth generations, Christians used any pretext to punish their Jewish neighbors with death for the supposed sins of their ancestors.

Large-scale anti-Semitism in the Christian world began in earnest during the Crusades. Although there was much in the Crusades that could be called romantic, there was little that was noble. It was in the fervor of the Crusades that Christians began to shed Jewish blood in payment for alleged Blood Libel supposedly divinely ordained for the Jews' crime of deicide.

The first accusations of Blood Libel appeared in Norwich, England, in 1144. Even before the concept of Blood Libel reared its unholy head, however, crusading European Christian armies were taking a bloody toll among the Jewish populations of Europe. During the First Crusade (1096-1099) Jews from the Rhenish provinces were slaughtered as the crusaders marched through the Rhine Valley on their way to liberate Palestine from the heathen Moslems. Given the choice of death or forced baptism, many Jews chose death in the name of *kiddush ha-shem* (martyrdom for the sanctification of God's name). Christian marauders attacked the Jewish communities of Speyer, Worm, Mainz, Regenburg and Prague; over 5,000 Jews were slaughtered by the time the First Crusade ran its course.

The Second Crusade (1147-1149) was less bloody than the first, probably because of the stricter discipline enforced by the spiritual leader of the Christian army, St. Bernard de Clairvaux. Even so, *The Jewish Almanac* tells us that the newly created doctrine of Blood Libel brought death to hundreds; the entire Jewish population of one French city were burned at the stake to atone for their ancestors' supposed crimes.

The Third Crusade (1189-1192) again took a fearsome toll among Europe's Jewish communities. The most violent acts occured in England; the worst single-day losses occurred in York where one hundred fifty Jews took refuge from Christian mobs by hiding in the cellar of a castle. The 150 chose suicide over baptism, and were dead before the mobs smashed through the heavy, copper-clad oaken doors to the inner keep.

The Crusades were a milestone in the deterioration of church-synagogue relations. It was during the Crusades that the word "Jew" first gained widespread popularity as a perjorative, being only rarely found in texts prior to 1000. At first, the term was used to indicate a merchant, and carried no perjorative meaning. It was also sometimes used in the variant form "Judaize" to denote those who wanted to make doctrinal or liturgical changes in the traditions of the Church, and eventually was applied to heretics as well (heretics were "Judaizers"). As the meaning of "Jew" changed, the merchant connotation became crooked or dishonest merchant, and the term was used as a racial or religious epithet. Even today, Christians and other gentiles sometimes use "Jew" as an epithet for dishonest businessmen, and not just dishonest Jewish businessmen; we sometimes talk of "Jewing down" the price of a merchant. While such usage rarely springs from malice aforethought, the primary criterion of malignancy, it nevertheless echos the murderous sentiments of our ancestors. Gentiles should use the word "Jew" cautiously and with thoughtful consideration of possible injury—even if it be inadvertent.

In 1236 the church took a stand against Judaism by attacking the *Talmud,* the principal code of Jewish law. A vengeful convert from Judaism named Nicholas Donin prepared a list of charges against the *Talmud* and presented them to Pope Gregory IX. Among

Donin's claims were charges that the *Talmud* attacked the Church and blasphemed both the Church's origins and Christ. Donin further pointed out to the Pope that chances of making converts among the Jews were small so long as the Jewish community revered the *Talmud* as equal to Scripture in importance.

After a short period of consideration, Pope Gregory sent a letter to the kings of Spain, France, Portugal and England, as well as to church officials throughout all of Europe, ordering that Jewish books be confiscated. The deed was carried out on the first Saturday in Lent, 1236—a date selected because most Jews would be in their synagogues. The books were confiscated and publicly burned. Doubtless few of the soldiers who made the seizures were Hebrew scholars, so many copies of the *Torah* (which we call the Old Testament) were burned in the same fires as the *Talmud*.

The most famous of the church's anti-Semitic spasms was the notorious Inquisition. Originally, the Inquisition had little to do with Jewish affairs and was merely the ecclesiastial court set up by the medieval church to stamp out the gnostic "Albigensian Heresy" (i.e. the Cathars) in southern France. The Inquisition eventually turned its wrath on the Jews, however, on the pretext that the Jews were the ultimate source of many extant heresies. The first mass executions of Jews under the Inquisition occurred in Troyes, France, in 1288 when Jews of the town were publicly burned at the stake for the crime of being Jewish.

The Spanish Inquisition started late (1480), but soon reached unparalleled heights of barbarity. Even today, the term "Spanish Inquisition" is often used erroneously as if the Inquisition existed solely on the Iberian Peninsula. For the first three years, the Spanish Inquisition was somewhat unremarkable, but in 1483 it attained substantial power under Tomas de Torquemada. The Grand Inquisitor of Spain enthusiastically rooted out heretics and put them to death. Heretics were tried in secret, so as to contain their heretical ideas, and then tortured, condemned and finally executed by burning at the stake in a festive public spectacle.

Under the Spanish Inquisition, tens of thousands of Jews were forced to choose conversion and baptism, or death and torture by some of the cruelest methods ever devised. Under that horrid regime there were many called *Moranos* or *Conversos,* i.e., Jews who submitted to baptism and nominally joined the church while maintaining their Jewish associations, beliefs and customs in secret. The *Conversos* were of special interest to the Inquisitor, and were repeatedly sought out and treated as heretics; many thousands were burned at the stake. The enthusiasm of the Inquisitors went to such extremes that they even exhumed the bodies of dead Jews and burned *them* at the stake also!

By 1492 authorities of the Spanish Inquisition had uncovered and murdered some 13,000 *Conversos,* plus numerous others. In the name of unifying the nation under one religion, it was decided that all Jews should be expelled from Spain. Because of this decision, it was difficult for Columbus to find seaworthy ships to make his voyage—it seems that Jewish communities were buying up most of the available vessels.

The expelled Iberian Jews wandered for several years trying to find permanent homes. Most of them settled in the Netherlands (which had been under Spanish rule), while small bands reportedly tried to settle on the west coast of Africa and in the mid-Atlantic Azore and Canary Islands. After the discovery of the New World, a band tried to settle in Portuguese Brazil. They were tolerated for a while, but were eventually expelled from there also. The wanderers from Brazil settled in the Dutch colony of New Amsterdam (present-day New York City). The Iberian Jews presented a perplexing problem for the Governor-General of the Dutch colony. It seems that the company's charter required all inhabitants to be members of the Dutch Reform (Protestant) church. Like any good company bureaucrat, the Governor wrote to corporate headquarters in Holland for instructions. Their practical reply ordered the Governor to ". . . not inquire too narrowly into their religious practices, for they are a hard-working and thrifty people of obvious benefit to the colony." The tormented Iberian wanderers finally found a home in the land that was to become the United States.

The word "pogrom" is guaranteed to evoke uneasiness among Jewish people, especially those of Eastern European or Russian origin. "Pogrom" is derived from the Russian word for "devastation," and graphically reminds us of what befell the Jews of heavily Christian Eastern European countries. The most recent wave of pogroms occurred within the memory of people still alive today (1881-1921), and sparked the massive Russian Jewish emigration to the United States at the turn of the century.

The Russian pogroms of 1881-1921 occurred in three waves: 1881-84, 1903-06 and 1917-21. These murderous torrents of vitriol coincided with Russian political crises. The 1881 attacks were occasioned by the assassination of Czar Alexander II, which the government quickly blamed on the Jews corporately. The second wave was sparked by the failed 1903-05 Russian revolution and the war with Japan in the Far East. During these troubles, the government diverted the revolutionary fervor of the people from the government to the Jews. The third wave resulted from the Bolshevik Revolution of 1917 which propelled the Communists to power, and by the civil war that followed the revolution. the pogroms did not abate until Communist strongman Josef Stalin put an end to them in 1921, and they did not reappear in any significant measure until German murder squads were aided in their work by native populations during the campaign of 1941-42 in the Ukraine.

It was been estimated that between 60,000 and 100,000 Jews were murdered during the forty years of pogroms between 1881 and 1921, and many tens of thousands more were robbed of their material goods, injured and mutilated; all within the memory of people still living today!

More often than not, local peasants and troops of the government were spurred on by the religious zeal of Russian Orthodox church authorities; once again the myth of Blood Libel exacted a gruesome toll among the Jewish people.

What good is served by dragging out the long and uncomfortable litany of past sins committed by nominally Christian people against the Jews? We gentile Christians know that no true, born-again Christian would harm the Jews, or even wish them ill. But that is not the point; what matters are Jewish perceptions of the situation. To the Jew, the long road to Auschwitz is paved with the bones of martyrs who died at the hands of men following the cross. From the crosses sewn on Crusader tunics to the Crucifix of the Grand Inquisitor to the twisted crosses on the armbands of SS murderers, the symbol of the cross—an ancient gallows used for executions—has haunted the Jewish people.

Christians in the Protestant tradition are sometimes prone to labeling Christian anti-Semitism as a Catholic phenomenon. We want to pin the blame for past sins on the Roman Catholic and Eastern Orthodox churches. It may truly be a catholic problem, but with a lower-case c in which "catholic" means *universal.*

The comfortable hypocrisy that Christian anti-Semitism is not a Protestant problem is too easily refuted by a brief look at the facts. From the time of Martin Luther until modern times there has been anti-Semitism and Jew-hatred among Protestants. During the twelve years of Nazi reign, loyalty to Adolf Hitler and devotion to Nazi dogma was deeper among Protestant Germans than among Catholics—despite the fact that Hitler and many top Nazis were born Catholic.

There are, however, signs that Christian attitudes towards the Jews are changing. Among evangelical

Protestants there are growing numbers of people who are very much pro-Israel, and who offer support and prayer for that nation.

Pope John XXIII brought about significant changes in those Roman Catholic practices which the Jews found most objectionable. Pope John has been called the "Jewish Pope," and is credited with saving the lives of numerous Jews who escaped to Turkey during the Holocaust. It was as Papal Nuncio in Turkey that John XXIII, then known as Cardinal Roncalli, aided Jewish escapees in their attempts to reach Palestine. Excitement rippled through the press when Pope John XXIII greeted a Jewish delegation with the words from Genesis 45:4—"I am Joseph, your brother." John XXIII reworded the Roman Catholic liturgy to eliminate certain phrases that carried anti-Semitic overtones, especially the phrase *pro perfidis judaeis.*

Following John's Vatican II conference, the Roman Catholic church issued a positively worded "Declaration on the Jews," a document often attributed to Cardinal Augustin Bea. The Cardinal undertook an analysis of New Testament Scripture to determine the church's proper attitude toward the Jews. From his study, Cardinal Bea concluded:

1. Scripture does not mark the Jews as deicides;

2. New Testament Scripture blames only those individuals who were directly involved with the Crucifixion; and

3. There can be no collective guilt for the Crucifixion.

By now, we should understand at least some of the reasons why Jewish people are naturally resistant to our Christian message; it is because their past experience gives them ample reason to fear us!

Gentile Christians have no clear idea what Judaism is and what makes someone or something Jewish. Most of us have a hazy idea of who were the Jews of biblical times, and erroneously assume a cultural continuity between ancient and modern Judaism so short as to make the Jews of today virtually identical to the Jews of the first century. We also tend to err in our assumption that Pharisaical Judaism of the New Testament defines all Jewish factions of that century.

So we have at least two disconnects in our gentile assumptions concerning Judaism: modern versus ancient Judaism and the monolithicity of Judaism in the first century. Perhaps it is time that we dispensed with unexamined assumptions and shed what light is required to illuminate them with truth.

In regard to that latter assumption, we can note that first-century Israel was split into numerous religious and political factions. Even the Pharisees were split into not fewer than seven factions arranged loosely around the schools of two major teachers: Rabbi Hillel and Rabbi Gamaliel.

Besides the Pharisees and Sadducees, there were the "Prophetic" or "Apocalyptic" Jews, the Essenes, the Gnostics (whose religion was tainted with teachings from Babylon) and the Zealots. The Prophetic Jews placed great emphasis on the prophets and their writings, and were especially interested in the Messianic prophecies. The Prophetic party had little

166

interest in the Pharisaical sacrificial cult of temple worship and instead prefered an ascetic life of holiness and purity. The prophetically oriented Jews had little use for the rote learning so highly prized by the Pharisees. The Essenes and Gnostics (which some believe were different manifestations of the same party) were also concerned with a life of holiness, and took that belief to the extreme of withdrawing from society. The Essenes tended to live in desert communities, one of which was apparently near the caves at Qumram where the Dead Sea Scrolls were found. The Zealots were less religious than nationalistic, and were constantly ready to wage war against the Romans.

These parties appear to have originated in the second century B.C., after the Maccabean Revolt which deposed Antiochus IV Epiphanes. The Pharisees placed strong emphasis on the doctrine of separation. Although not as strong as the Essenes' separation ideas, and possibly derived from Scriptural warrant, the separation doctrine led to such pride over being the Chosen People that many of them forgot that to be chosen by God means a call to be a holy people as well.

Pharisaical Judiasm was ill-equipped for the coming of the Messiah because their separatist doctrine taught them to look for a strictly Jewish Messiah sent only for the Jewish people—the separated Chosen People. Furthermore, centuries of foreign domination caused them to hope for the victorious Messiah of Scripture who would free Israel politically from gentile domination. Overlooked was the suffering Messiah seen in the Scriptures.

The nature of Judaism had to change radically after A.D. 70 when the Roman army under Titus destroyed the Temple at Jerusalem. Sacrificial worship was no longer possible after the Temple ceased to exist. During the final campaign of the revolt, the Romans slaughtered 600,000 Jews and carried a like number into slavery. Roman victory was so complete that another half century was to pass before a remnant of Jews again tried to revolt against Rome. The A.D. 70 victory so elated Titus' father, Emperor Vespasian, that he issued a special set of commemorative coins called by collectors today the *Judea Capta* series.

The catastrophe was so great that it changed Jewish culture and forced it into the avenues of history which created modern Judaism. Rabbinic Judaism seems to have developed from antecedents within Pharisaical Judaism as a temporary measure for a relatively short exile. What was intended to last only a short time until restoration, however, has become firmly entrenched as tradition: it was to be 1,878 years before the restoration began!

Gentile persecution of the Jewish people was not a strictly Christian phenomenon, and did not originate in the Christian era after Christianity became the official state religion of Rome, but began even before the Roman legions put down the first revolt of A.D. 66-70. Indeed, Christians at that time were also a persecuted minority under Rome; the blood of our first martyrs had only recently soaked into the Coliseum ground when Titus sacked Jerusalem.

Rabbinic Judaism continued the Pharisees' separation doctrine not just from religious considerations, but developed it further in order to ensure mere survival in an increasingly uncertain and anti-Semitic world. Thus we find strong evidence that many of the attitudes and doctrines of Rabbinic Judaism were apparently designed to prevent assimilation of the Jewish people with surrounding populations. And it seems to have worked, for the Jewish communities of the world have remained separate and identifiable through nineteen centuries of persecution.

Oddly enough, many modern Jewish writers fail to distinguish any difference of importance between post-revolt Rabbinic Judaism as we know it today and pre-revolt Pharisaical Judaism. They are partially correct, of course, because modern rabbinism developed slowly with the changing needs of the community.

After the persecutions of the Christian era began in earnest, rabbinical Judaism became more and more dependent upon negating Christianity because an affirmation of Christian belief was tantamount to encouraging assimilation. By the time of the Crusades—a full millenium after the birth of Jesus—Christianity was totally gentile, and there was little with which the Jewish community could identify. To adopt Christian Messianic doctrine meant a dissolution of Rabbinic Judaism, which by that time had become a vested interest.

In modern usage, the word "Judaism" means not just biblical Judaism, Pharisaical Judaism and the 613 precepts of rabbinic Judaism, but also factors that even totally secularized non-religious Jews can accept: folklore, culture, Jewish customs and traditions, and a uniquely Jewish ethos. I can recall speaking with a young Jewish woman at George Washington University in Washington, D.C. She had transferred into that formerly Presbyterian school that semester, and was elated because "at this school one can be *so Jewish* and nobody minds!" Yet that same woman only moments before bragged that she had not been inside a synagogue since she was fourteen years old. So what does "Judaism" mean to her? I don't know, but a Jewish friend of mine affirmed that "Jewishness" was a "race, religion, nationality, culture and state of mind interacting in a hopelessly complex way that we ourselves don't understand." In fact, he claimed, if you ask two Jews the question "What is Jewishness?" at the same time, you are likely to get four good answers and ten new questions.

The charge is often leveled at Hebrew Christians that they have lost their "Jewishness" by turning their backs on Judaism, in essence becoming traitors to their own people. Their problem is exacerbated by the assumptions of some gentile Christians that all new Christians have to become carbon copies of themselves and fit into the White Anglo-Saxon Protestant mold. Many are the Christian missionaries and evangelists who have tried to force-fit new converts into some rigid WASP denominational role to ill effect.

The non-Christian Jewish people must be convinced that there are no historical, cultural or theological grounds for the claim that Hebrew Christians (or "Messianic Jews" as some prefer to be called) have abandoned their Jewishness. It may be true that they have abandoned certain teachings of rabbinism, but Judaism is still very much the love of their hearts.

The phenomenon of Jewish Christianity is not a new religion as some would have us believe, but rather a reaffirmation of old Jewish doctrines and tenets. The Messianic Jew is merely a Jew of a different sort. We hear of four major divisions within modern Judaism: reconstructionist (secularist), reform, conservative and orthodox. Perhaps sometime in the near future it will become fashionable to talk of a fifth major division: Messianic Judaism. No longer will the Hebrew Christian have to feel embarrassed to admit to other Jewish people that he or she belongs to a *Beth Messiah* congregation.

Gentile Christians will have to re-examine some of their own ideas regarding Jewish Christians. The teaching that God is finished with the Jewish people because they corporately rejected Christ (a charge that needs some close scrutiny!) is *false teaching.* Similarly, in our repentance we must also give up the cherished notion that God's promises and covenants with Israel now apply exclusively to the Church—called "spiritual Israel" in order to not torture Scripture—and not to the Jewish people. The major problem with the latter doctrine is that it logically requires God to be a liar, and since it is not God who is the liar, one can only wonder at the author of that doctrinal error. Our insistence on these twin doctrines is like a petulant younger brother who hopes mightily that the older, albeit prodigal, brother will not return to father's house.

We must be willing to allow Hebrew Christians the freedom to follow their own customs, ritual, liturgy and methods of worshiping God. *There is not one word of Scripture anyplace in the Bible that requires Jews to stop being Jews when they accept the Messiah.* Jewish worship customs are not offensive to God, so they should not be offensive to us.

One of the many factors contributing to Jewish and Christian misunderstanding of one another is definitions of terms. Even when we speak to each other, communications often fail for the lack of a common understanding of words. Let's examine some of those misunderstandings.

One word that carries unnecessary emotional baggage for Jews is "convert." To many Jewish people, the convert to Christianity has betrayed Jewish heritage because conversion implies changing one's religion. In the past, this unfortunate connotation was validated by the fact that the convert soon stopped attending synagogue and started attending a gentile church; modern-day Messianic synagogues are, after all, a recent phenomenon. But does the Jewish convert to Christianity actually change his or her religion? No, for Christianity is a Jewish offspring that temporarily went entirely gentile. All of the original church members were Jewish, and Jesus himself was an observant Jew living in a Jewish community.

It becomes difficult to separate Judaism from Christianity when one studies the first-century Church. In essence, Christianity is intensely Jewish. Is not the Jew who becomes a Christian merely acting in accordance with Scriptures that predicted the Messiah? So who's the "convert"?

A Jewish person cannot "convert" to Christianity because Christianity is Jewish! It is the gentile Christian who in a sense converted to Judaism the instant he accepted Jesus—an orthodox first-century Jew—as Savior and Messiah.

Many Jewish people believe that all non-Jews in the Western nations are "Christians." They erroneously assume that Christians are born into the religion; they, after all, were born Jewish. It may seem strange to them that all Christians are essentially converts, which in this case implies a turning toward God, a change of heart and not necessarily religion.

It also seems strange to them that not all church-goers are Christians (that one really confuses!). The phrase "born again" is meaningless prattle to them because the concept, until explained, is foreign.

Another fracture in the disconnected jawbone of Jewish-Christian dialogue is the symbol of the cross, a theme introduced earlier. Christians with a mission and a burden for Jewish evangelism would do well to eliminate the symbol of the cross from their message, while retaining the substance of the message that the symbol represents. A seminarian friend of mine discussed this subject with me, and he scolded me that we could not eliminate the "doctrine of the cross." *There is no doctrine of the cross!* There is only the doctrine of the *substitutionary death of Christ for the atonement of our sins.* The cross is the mere symbol of that atoning act, not its substance. The use of the cross can frighten Jewish people because of cultural scars from crimes perpetrated by men who marched and lived under the sign of the cross. To the Jewish person, the cross is a gallows on which the lives of thousands of forebears were sacrificed.

So why not eliminate the cross from our Gospel message? We have, after all, not one hint of Scriptural warrant for our use of the cross as a symbol. If it offends our Jewish friends to the point of harming the Gospel message, then let's not use it. Besides, many Christians cherish symbols such as neckchain crosses and magnificent *Christus Rex* statues over altars almost to the point of idolatry and thereby deteriorate their spiritual experience.

As a side issue, let's address the matter of jewelry that superimposes a cross on a Star of David. The intent of the wearer is admirable, for they wish to express our debt to the Jews as the foundation of our religion. But despite the good intentions of the wearers, I cannot conceive of a more effective way to offend some Jewish people. Perhaps a good alternative is to wear the type of jewelry in which a dove or lamb is superimposed on the Magen David—those symbols lack the negative evocative power of the cross.

My next suggestion could get me boiled in oil in some evangelical circles. The name *Jesus Christ* offends many Jewish people. Again, it is not the true followers of Jesus who caused the problem, but the murderous mobs pretending to act in His name. Horrible memories are evoked when the words "Jesus" or "Christ" are uttered in the presence of Jewish people who are aware of their own (recent) history. So let's not use the words "Jesus" or "Christ" when witnessing to Jewish people. I can hear the angry protests already! But before you reach for the tar pot and feather bag, hear me out, for there is a solution to the problem.

It is not the *name* of Christ which is the problem, it is the *words* "Jesus" and "Christ." We must be aware of the origin of those words and communicate those origins to the Jewish people. "Jesus" is an English transliteration of a Greek transliteration of a Hebrew name: *Yeshua*. Secondly, "Christ" is an English transliteration of the Greek "Christos," which is translated *Há Mashiach* ("messiah") in Hebrew. The English words "Jesus Christ," therefore, could be rendered *Yeshua Ha' Mashiach* in Hebrew. Perhaps re-Judaizing Jesus will be less disturbing to the Jewish people. Besides, it is technically correct to use the Hebrew version.

But there is a pitfall in bending over backwards in order to not offend. While it is always proper and polite to use terminology that does not offend, we must not fall prey to the trap of separating Jesus from His Gospel. It is never proper to hide Jesus in *Yeshua*—always make it perfectly clear that it is Jesus who is being discussed. Otherwise, you will be little more than a manipulator and deceiver, despite your honorable intent.

Numerous Jewish writers have marvelled at the character of Jesus once they managed to overcome the distortions wrought by false Christians. When those writers examined what Jesus actually said, rather than the oblique interpretations of what some churchman said He said, then the germ of truth will begin to sprout and may yet bring forth much fruit. Unfortunately, the sprout is oftentimes left to wilt like a Jericho Rose for the lack of water and nourishment.

Surprisingly, few Jewish writers on Jesus or the New Testament relate the subject to the Old Testament. That is such a shame! For it is from the Old Testament (which one Jewish friend likes to call the "Only Testament") that we gain our deepest insight into the mission of Jesus, the manner of His coming and both the reasons for, and manner of, His death.

We learn from the Jewish system of substitutionary death (sacrifices) for the atonement of sin, evident in Jewish culture as far back as Abraham, just why Jesus had to be executed. The person of Jesus is identified in the Messianic prophecies of the Old Testament down to the last detail, even the date of his death according to some scholars.

Any examination of either testament without the other puts on blinders that hide the whole truth. Taken together, the Old and New Testaments form a harmonious synergism—a whole greater than the sum of its parts—which is denuded of essential vitality if either is missing.

Just as sad as the Jewish person who reads the New Testament outside of the context of the Old is the Christian who tries to witness Christ to Jewish people in a strictly New Testament frame of reference. Do not forget that the New Testament is an alien document to the Jewish people, so its authority is not established with them: *it is not accepted as Scripture.* An effective witness will start with the Old Testament and then progress to show the harmony of the Old and New Testaments—they form a continuum. I favor tearing out the title page between *Malachi* and *Matthew* because it seems to form a brick wall to understanding —a point of discontinuity that makes it easy for nonbelievers to stop studying.

The Splitting

There is a great parenthesis in the timeline of Christian evangelism among Jewish people. During the first decade of Church history there was no question of Jewish evangelism because the membership was almost exclusively Jewish and all of the evangelists were Jewish. Virtually all evangelism in the first few years was among Jewish communities resident in Greek and Roman cities; the first place a Christian evangelist went when entering a new town was the local synagogue.

It usually comes as a surprise to modern Jewish people to find out that the first really serious doctrinal dispute in the Church was over *whether or not to admit gentiles,* and if they were admitted, under what terms and conditions. One faction of the Jerusalem church held that gentile converts to Christianity had to undergo the same process and ritual cleansing *as any other convert to Judaism,* including circumcision for males. To the all-Jewish protochurch of the first century, there was no separation from Judaism.

The faction that prevailed in the Jerusalem dispute held that gentile converts did not have to undergo the ceremonial process of becoming Jewish. It is in that early decision that we find the seeds of the eventual Jewish-gentile Christian split.

The word "Christian" connotes "gentile" among Jewish people. The denotation, however, is "follower of Jesus Christ," and to the Church fathers, the word did not carry any implication of either Jewish or gentile followers—just followers of Jesus Christ no matter what the stripe.

Even though the process of splitting began shortly after the Roman victory in A.D. 70, and was re-confirmed by the Roman victory in A.D. 135, there were considerable contacts between Jewish and gentile Christians for several hundred years. It was not until after Christians came to wield political power that persecution of the Jews could begin in earnest: anti-Semitism before the time of Constantine the Great was little more than disorganized bombast from a few Jew-haters who knew how to write. Until that time, there were three main strands of Judean influence on the religious life of the Western world: Rabbinic Judaism, Messianic Judaism and gentile Christianity. By the fifth century, however, Messianic Jewish synagogues had largely disappeared and Christianity became all but exclusively gentile.

The demise of the messianic synagogues may not have been due to a lack of vitality, or pressures from other Jewish communities. Their fall was due to anti-Semitism in the gentile church, to be sure, but there is a strong possibility that the whole scene was orchestrated. There seems to be no plausible reason for the fall of Messianic Judaism at that time, especially when both Jew and Christian were enjoying tolerance in the empire for the first time in centuries. Dr. Malachai Martin is a former Jesuit priest who served in the Vatican, and who is an expert on Church history. In his book *The Decline and Fall of the Roman Church* he records the relationship between the Jewish and gentile churches at the time of Constantine. The first Pope under the authority of the Roman government was Silvester. After he consolidated his power by defeating the Donatist sect, he turned his attentions to the Jewish church. The issue was not merely that the Jewish churches were the oldest in all of Christendom, but also that most of them were ruled by *Desposyni* who were descendents from the immediate family of Jesus. To Silvester and succeeding Popes, these *Desposyni* represented a force fundamentally different from his own who could possibly seize control of the church. The Popes were only then consolidating their power over other bishops, and did not need competitors who had both the authority inherent in the oldest churches in Christendom and blood relationship to Jesus. It appears that Silvester and his followers may have instituted anti-Semitic policies in order to rid themselves of potential competitors for power within the Church!

Jewish evangelism went into further eclipse after the end of the Roman era, and did not reappear until the 18th century in, of all places, Germany. And it was not the false sword-point evangelism of the Inquisition and the Crusades, but rather a heart-felt effort of people who really loved God's Chosen People in the manner He intended. No longer were Christian attempts to present the Gospel to Jewish people made in the spirit of *adversus judaeos,* but in a spirit of love and goodwill. It was only a few generations from the beginnings of Jewish evangelism in Germany until Hitler rose to power and became the ultimate adversary of the Jewish people.

The Holocaust presented the Church with a unique opportunity to examine its own sins and to repent of them. In some inexplicable manner, the Church contributed to Hitler's rise and success by its own pride—which led to abetting the Nazis. The Holocaust shocked many Christians into rebuking their personal and corporate anti-Semitism, thereby setting the stage for evangelism among the Jewish people. It has been estimated that more Jewish people have come to accept Jesus as Messiah since 1967 than in the previous 1,500 years! The Messianic movement among the Jewish people is stronger now than in any recent century. Perhaps one of the most exciting signs of the End Times is that Jewish people can now hear the Gospel from Jewish lips in a uniquely Jewish context that no gentile can mimic.

The Righteous Gentiles provide us with an object lesson in how we should react to the Jews. They provide us with a lesson in elementary Christian love and in basic ethics. It is time that we learned those lessons well, for there may well be a next time.

Selections for Further Reading

The story of the Holocaust, or even just the smaller story of the Righteous Gentiles, is too large for any one book. For those who wish to study the subject further the author recommends the following books.

1. Altshuler, David (editor), *The Precious Legacy: Judiac Treasures from the Czechoslovak State Collections,* Smithsonian Traveling Exhibition Service, published by Summit Books (New York, 1983). This book is available in both soft and hard covers, and is the official catalog of the Smithsonian traveling exhibition of the same name.

2. Carr, Joseph J.; *The Twisted Cross,* Huntington House (Shreveport, LA, 1985). This book details the New Age Movement occultic connections of Hitler and other top Nazis.

3. Cumbey, Constance; *Hidden Dangers of the Rainbow,* Huntington House (Shreveport, LA, 1984). Mrs. Cumbey reveals the modern New Age Movement and provides details similar to the selection above regarding Hitler.

4. Eliach, Yaffa; *Hasidic Tales of the Holocaust,* Oxford University Press (New York, 1982). The ultra-orthodox Hasidic Jews of Eastern Europe used the tale as a means of teaching and communicating lessons on morals, ethics, history, etc. This book relates some of the tales from the Holocaust. Must reading for any who are interested in Jewish culture.

5. Friedlander, Saul; *Kurt Gerstein: The Ambiguity of Good,* Alfred A. Knopf, Publishers (New York, 1969).

6. Glatstein, Jacob and Israel Knox (editors); *Anthology of Holocaust Literature,* Atheneum Books (New York, 1980). A collection of pieces written about or during the Holocaust. This book, along with Hallie (see below) was the source of the story on Pastor Trocmé.

7. Gutman Yisrael and Efraim Zuroff; *Rescue Attempts During the Holocaust,* Yad Vashem Publication (Jerusalem, 1977). This book contains the proceedings of a meeting held in Jerusalem and presents much original material.

8. Hallie, Philip; *Lest ʼInnocent Blood Be Shed,* Harper & Row/Colophon Books (San Francisco, 1980). This book was the principal source of the story on Pastor Trocmé and is must reading for anyone interested in the Righteous Gentiles or Christian ethics in situations such as the Holocaust; a superb job of writing.

9. Hellman, Peter; *The Avenue of the Righteous,* Atheneum Books (New York, 1980). This book was the principal source for the stories of the Henry family and Mademoiselle Chaumat and of Sietske Postma. Hellman is a sensitive and talented writer whose accounts make one feel as if he actually knows the characters involved. Another "must reading" for students of the Holocaust or the Righteous Gentiles.

10. *Yad Vashem Bulletin* and other publications of Yad Vashem Heroes and Martyrs Remembrance Authority, Jerusalem, Israel. The list of publications is too long for reprinting here, but the reader can obtain a copy directly from Yad Vashem, P.O. Box 3477, Jerusalem.

Roll Call of the Righteous

Partial listing of persons who have won the Righteous Gentile Award, issued by Yad Vashem, Jerusalem, Israel.

AUSTRIA
Oswald Bosko
Ewald and Danuta Kleisinger
Ludwig and Maria Knapp
Hermann Langbein
Julius Madritsch
Julius Nataly
Johann Pscheidt
Anton Schmid
Raimund Titsch
Dr. Leo Tschöll

BELGIUM
Robert and Blanche Jowa
Elisabeth La Reine
Franz and Rosa Lemmens
Monseigneur André Meunier
Ivonne Feyerick Nevejean
Leopold Ros
Antoon and Julia Visser

BULGARIA
Dimo Kazasov

CZECHOSLOVAKIA
Dr. Anna Binder-Urbanova
Jan and Maria Caraj

Karel Frydl
Vaclav Juran
Michal and Maria Jancik
Ljudevit Kacir and Family
Przemisl Piter
Josef Rîha
Sara Schalkhaz
Margit Schlachta
Karl Simoncic
Jan Tkadlecek
Anton Trokan

DENMARK
Anna Christensen

ENGLAND
Charles Coward

FRANCE
Louise Blazer
Raymond Carbonnet
Emile Carpentier
Monseigneur Chalve
Mme. G. Chesneau
Suzan Davy
Jean Deffaught
Abbé Jean Fleury

Marinette Guy
Dr. Adelaide Hautval
Catherine Krafft
Père Pierre Maria-Benoit
Blanche Molino
Simone Mourier
Family Oesch
Pierre and Denise Renard
Germaine Ribière
Marguerite Soubeyran
Juliette Vidal

GERMANY
Elisabeth Abegg
Richard Abel
Bernhard Falkenberg
Theodor Görner
Hermann Grabe
Propst Dr. Heinrich Grüber
Eberhard Helmrich
Werner Krume
Maria Letnar
Dr. Gertrud Luckner
Prälat Dr. Hermann Maas
Josef Mayer
Paul Mayer
Roza Mayer
Ernst-Bruno Motzko
Karl Schörghofer and Family
Konrad Schwesser
Hans Walz
Armin Wegner
Irmgard Wieth
Ludwig Woerl

GREECE
Helene Capart
Maria Choleva
Monseigneur Damaskinos
Angelos Evert
Metropolit Genadios
Michail Glykas
Kleopatra Mino
Dimitrios Vranopoulus

HOLLAND
Dionysius and Cornelia Bakker

Jo and Anne Bakker
Jan and Gé Blokker
Johannes Bogard
Theo and Wilhemina Bol
Family Breyer
Dr. Gerrit and Gerda
    Brillenburg-Wurth
Hylke and Jen Brug
Jo and Josephien De Geest
A.M. De Jong
Frederic Christian and
    Harmina De Mars
Hendrik and Hendrika De Mars
Jacobus and Adriana Den Hamer
Arnold Douwes
Willem and Alvina
    Driebergen-van Der Meiden
Cornelis and Louisa Drop
Family Flokstra
Isaac and Barbara Groenenberg
Hendrik Haizing
Anton and Lina Helmer
Johannes Hilderson
Maarten and Non Hulst
Andries and Jta Jansen
Elizabeth and Albert Klop
Albert and Aukie Koops
Cornelis and Sara Korver
Willem Kraan
Frans, Margarete and Sara
    Lammens
Cilia Loots
Meta Mayer
Truus Menger
Kurel and Nel Millard
Piet Nak
Miss Paré
Johanes Pieper
Gerardus Jacobus Pontier
Johannes and Dien Post
Jan and Tina Reitsema
Hannie Schaft
Joo and Beb Scholten
Afke and Tine Sieswerda
Simon Spinder and Family
Hyme and Emelie Stoffels

Adela Teebom
Dr. Anton Tellegen
Henrietta Tellegen
Corrie Ten Boom
Barend and Suzanne Van Beek
Theo and Beth Van Dalen
Ali Van Der Geld
Jan and Jo Van Der Helm
Willem Jan and
    Johanna Van Der Linden
Gerard and Molly Van Heel
Arie Van Mansum
Dr. Wilhelmus and Dr. Joanna-
    Maria Van Meuwen
Hermine Van Skepele
Gerardus Johannes Van't Vlie
Johanna and Ronkje Venema
Dr. Joor and Nike Verhey
Wim and Sitje Verschoor
Emmy Verwoerd
Cornelis and Amanda Vissers
Joop and Willy Westerweel
Gertrud Wijsmuller-Meyer

HUNGARY
Charles-Károly Horváth
    and Family
Barna Kiss
Wilmos Nagy-Baconyi Nagy
Imre Revicky
Imre Szabó
Laszló Szabó
István Vasdényey
Andor Zsoldos

ITALY
Don Arrigo Beccari
Alfonso Canova
Don Letto Casini
Sale Dante
Odoardo Focherini
Ezio Giorgetti
Prof. Carlo Arturo Jemolo
Dr. Giuseppe Moreali
Mario and Lina Santerini
Don Giovanni Simioni

Prof. Angelo Della Torre
Don Giuseppe De Zotti

NORWAY
Ingebjorg Fostyedt-Sletten

POLAND
Maria Adamowska
Mark Arczynski
Helena Arwaniti
Wladyslaw Bartoszewski
Bogdan Bazil
Piotr and Stanislawa Bieganski
Stanislaw and Zofia Boczkowski
Karol Bogucki
Janina Buchholz
Piotr Budnik
Szymon Celka
Eduard Chacze
Pawel Charmuszko
Wladyslawa Choms
Jan Cieply
Romualda and Feliks Ciesielska
Stanislaw and Anna Ciesla
Stefania Cimiega
Feliks Cywinski
Stanislawa Demska
Wiktoria Diedzic-Skrzypiec
Maria Drydal-Kelbasa
Waclaw and Leonia Egermaier
Wanda Filopowicz
Yosef Fink and Wife
Antoni Fularski
Bronislawa and Julian Gawelczyk
Stefan Glinka
Mariana Gut
Wladyslaw Grzegorczyk
Dr. Pawel Horbaczewski
Olena Hryhoryshyn
Franciszka Hupale
Henryk Iwanski
Wiktoria Iwanski
Staszek Jackow
Vaclaw and Marcelina Jacyna
Jan and Janina Jamiolkowksi
Helena and Boleslaw Janc

Juliana Jasinska-Larych
Wladyslaw Jaskolska
Brygida Kafar
Jan and Magda Kakol
Procailo Kalwinski
Felix Kanbus
Stanislawa Karsov Szymaniewska
Zofia Katarsyna Rozen
Sofia Klemens
Mikolaj and Karolina Kmita
Piotr, Karolina and
   Mieczyslaw Kobylec
Josefa Korniecka
Maria and Witold Kowalski
Wladyslaw Kowalski
Stanislaw Krzemienski
Irena Kucharzek
Keopolda Kuropiecka
Veronika Kwiadaras
Janis and Johanna Lipke
Pelagja Lozinska
Suzanna Lozinska
Ignancy Lubczynski
Wojcieh Maciejko
Bronislawa Majewska
Rozalia Makara
Jan Mikulski and Family
Stefan and Marcela Miller
Wladyslaw Misiuna
Ogonowski Family
Apolonia an dAleksander Oldak
Jan Pawlicki
Franciszek Pekalski
Sofia Persiak
Josef and Zofia Pietrowski
Bronislawa Plaskarz
Wladyslaw Podworski
Franciszek and Barbara Polewka
Witold Pominko
Genia Pukaite
Stefan Raczynski
Lucia Reicher Galikowska
Henryk Rolirad
Aleksander Roslan
Dionizy Roswandowski
Zygmunt Rytel

Sylwia Rzeczycka
Kazimiera Sadzikowska
Maria Sawicka
Irena Sendler
Stefan Siewierski
Stanislaw and Halina Slebiecka
Stefan Sobala
Maria Sobecka
Stanislaw Sobczak
Josef Socha
Zofia Sokolowska
Sygmund and Dr. Wiktoria
   Struszinski
Kazimierz Szelagowski
Helena Szemet
Witold Szymczukiewicz
Dr. Andrej Trojanowski–
Ignac Ustianowski
Anna Wachalska
Antoni Werstler
Tadeusz Wiatr
Izydor and Jaroslawa Wolosianski
Stanislaw Woloszyn
Dr. Jan and Antonia Zabinski
Eva Zajac
Boleslaw Zawadzki
Janusz Zwolakowski
Josef and Franka Zwonarz

PORTUGAL
Aristides de Sousa Mendes

RUMANIA
Traian Popovici

SWEDEN
Waldemar and Nina Langlet
Raoul Wallenberg

SWITZERLAND
Charles Lutz

U.S.S.R.
Ukraine
Antonia Gabis
Machail Jaciuk
Fjodor Michailovitch-Kalenchuk

Lithuania
Sofia Beinkine
Vladas Krusinkas
Ona Simaite
Julia Bronislavovna
    Vitkauskene

Estonia
Prof. Uko Masing

YUGOSLAVIA
Bartulovic Olga and Dragica
Pavao Horvat
Nemanja Jovanovic and Family
Stanko and Ljubinka Jovanovic
Dr. Miroslaw Stojadinovic